Retriever Training

Retriever Training

The Modern Way

by

Susan Scales

David & Charles

Newton Abbot   London   North Pomfret (Vt)   Vancouver

ISBN 0 7153 5246 7
Library of Congress Catalog Card Number 76-40808

Set in 11 on 13pt English
and printed in Great Britain
by Biddles Ltd, Guildford, Surrey
for David & Charles (Publishers) Limited
Brunel House Newton Abbot Devon

Published in the United States of America
by David & Charles Inc
North Pomfret Vermont 05053 USA

Published in Canada
by Douglas David & Charles Limited
1875 Welch Street North Vancouver BC

Contents

Firstly, to the distinguished trainers named in this book, without whose willing help it could not have been written.

Secondly, to the host of other amateurs and professionals for whose help and advice on many occasions I am deeply grateful.

Thirdly, to all the good friends I have made with a common interest in gundogs.

Fourthly, to my husband who took the photographs.

Finally, to Manymills Lucky Charm, W.T.Ch. Manymills Tanne and their descendants, to whom I owe the greatest debt of all.

1 First Thoughts before the First Pup

A working partnership with any animal brings its own special and unique rewards. This is particularly true in the case of dogs, with which man has had such a long and mutually advantageous relationship. In addition to the sheer delight of owning a trained dog, to the individual of the right mentality (it is hoped that the qualities necessary for successful ownership will become apparent later in this book), is the practical necessity for most shooting people to own an efficient gundog.

For the rough shooter, it is not to be denied that the most satisfactory choice of dog is almost certainly a spaniel, probably an English Springer. However, for those who do a lot of driven game shooting or wildfowling, a retriever of some sort is the obvious choice. For those who do both, there is a lot to be said for owning one of each breed, although some will prefer to teach their spaniels to sit quietly at drives and range out further for their retrieves than they are encouraged to do while hunting up game. Others will prefer to own a retriever and teach him, in addition to his normal duties, to act as a spaniel in hedgerow hunting and generally putting up game within shot. There is no doubt that this can be done, but success is far more likely to be achieved with a dog bred specifically for the job to be entrusted to it. However, those who wish to train a spaniel as a retriever or vice versa should proceed in exactly the same way as if they were training one of the more conventional breeds designed for the job.

For humane reasons it goes without saying that the lone wildfowler, or in fact anyone who shoots on his own, ought not to be without an efficient retriever to bring wounded game into the bag. It seems to worry some people far more if they fail to find a bird they were sure was dead than failing on a difficult runner. To me, however, the latter is worse. Although a bird which is barely wing-tipped may well recover and live to fly another day, and even broken legs often mend, the thought of leaving an injured bird to die slowly, if it is not mercifully found first by a fox, is abhorrent.

In these days of ever-increasing inflation and world food shortage, it is economically important to bring every bird or beast shot into the bag. It would be better to shoot clay pigeons than to shoot live birds and not make every effort to ensure that they are found and made use of by somebody, even if the shooter himself has no wish to eat them.

The only sort of game shooting for which no dog is necessary is the very formal grouse, partridge or pheasant shoot where ample picking-up dogs are provided, and where guns' own dogs are probably not even welcome. However, there must be few shooters whose sport consists exclusively of this sort of occasion, and many of them find as the years go by that they get more and more pleasure out of working their dogs and less and less out of the actual shooting.

Even so, if the reader should decide that he or she is not of the right temperament to own a dog, or circumstances do not allow him to keep one in a reasonable manner, it would be far better for him to do without and find some enthusiastic owner wanting work and experience for his dogs to accompany him on his shooting days.

Having decided that he ought to have a retriever and, even more important, that he would *like* to have one, the decision must be made as to what his choice should be. There are several approaches to the problem. Possibly the safest solution is to buy a trained adult of two to three years old. It is impossible for a dog younger than this to be fully trained as, although he might have completed his preliminary training course, he cannot have had a season's experience on the real

10

thing. However, this will entail laying out a large sum. How large can be calculated by adding up the weekly cost of the dog's food for two years, plus probable vet's bills, training expenses such as transport to various different types of cover and water, and something for the trainer's highly skilled time. A professional trainer will also have to add on something in the way of overheads and a contribution to the unsuccessful pupils he has had to sell at a loss. A cheap so-called trained dog is likely to be a very dubious purchase indeed, as there are few dog people nowadays who do not know the value of what they are selling. In any case, no one should buy a trained dog without a convincing demonstration of what it can do. Dogs with field trial awards are in a rather different category as they have proved their ability. They occasionally come on the market if they have developed some minor fault which renders them less valuable for trials, but they may be perfectly satisfactory for normal work.

When buying an adult trained dog it is extremely important to choose one with a temperament which suits his future handler. Anyone who has had experience of selling adult dogs will know the satisfaction to be gained from fitting a round peg into a round hole and supplying a buyer with a dog about which one will receive eulogistic reports for many years to come. It is important, therefore, for the potential buyer to be absolutely honest about the sort of person he is and the kind of life his dog will be expected to lead.

A method of dog acquisition which will probably work out no cheaper than the above in the long run, although the payments will be spread over a longer period of time, is to buy a puppy bred from the right sort of working stock and send it to a professional trainer when it is old enough. Thus the dog will already be settled into the household and will know (and, one hopes, love) his future owner. However, he will probably require at least a month to settle down in the trainer's kennels before anything much can be done with him, and therefore the training time will be longer by this period. Training fees are not cheap, as they have to cover not only the board of the dog (enquiry at any good boarding kennel will elicit the going price) but also skilled training time. Neither can the conscientious trainer accommodate nearly so many dogs at a time as the boarding kennel owner. There is, too, always the risk that the puppy will turn out to be a disappointment and all this time and money will have been wasted. However, with the right puppy of the right breeding, sent to a reputable trainer rather than one of the old 'boot and stick' brigade, the chances of success are high.

The most satisfying approach is undoubtedly to buy a puppy and train it oneself. It will be cheaper, but not as much cheaper as one might think. However, the dividends in terms of satisfaction and pleasure of having a really good dog which is all one's own work cannot be over stated. Added to which, a trained dog will always go better for his trainer than any other handler, no matter how skilled the latter might be. The owner-trainer will have more time to work on and overcome any snags that might occur, a professional being tempted to reject any pupil which faces him with serious problems, in order to produce quicker results from easier material.

Not everyone can train a dog, of course. Some would like to and may well be perfectly capable of doing so, but the circumstances of their lives or work make it impossible. However, many difficulties of this sort can be overcome, and many a gundog has received most of its training in a city park, with no detriment at all to the finished article. The more difficulties there are, the more ingenuity the trainer is going to bring to bear to overcome them, which is all to the good. I sometimes wonder if people lucky enough to have all the training facilities they want on their own premises are really so fortunate. Those of us who are forced to take our dogs out by car to different places to find different conditions may well end up with the better-educated dog, as he will have had more experience of life generally and will probably have spent more time out of the kennel and with the trainer.

Having made the decision to buy a puppy and train it oneself, it still has to be decided whether to buy a pup of eight weeks or so or an older one ready for training. A lot depends upon the time of year and how soon the would-be trainer hopes to have his dog ready to take out shooting, but generally speaking a good puppy of six to twelve months is very difficult to come by. It is not economic sense for a breeder to run on more than one or two puppies from each litter to this age, as they are very expensive to rear properly and are not worth a great deal of money before they have had any training. In addition, few people are in a position to give enough individual time to more than a very few dogs to ensure that their mental upbringing has been all that it should be. Nothing would induce me to buy a puppy of this age which had never been beyond the confines of its own kennel or had anything done to stimulate its intelligence.

Assuming that the breeder has kept one or two puppies for himself, questions should be asked if he suddenly decides to sell one just at the time he could start to do something with it. Of course, it is possible that he may have kept the two he liked best in order to defer his final choice. Then the buyer is probably being offered the second pick of litter, to which there could be no possible objection. Alternatively, a pup may have suddenly developed a fault, or the breeder may have decided that its temperament is not of the right sort. It should be pointed out, however, that the fact that the temperament is wrong for one person does not necessarily mean that it will be wrong for somebody else. The breeder may be the kind of person to whom the over-submissive 'let me lick your boots' type is anathema, but there are people for whom this characteristic in a dog would be just right.

Equally, there are circumstances under which the ideal young dog is available on the market through no fault of its own. The owner may have died or been posted abroad. There are numerous reasons why a good young dog can become available, sometimes even at a price less than it will have cost to rear to that age. However, the prospective purchaser must be prepared to be patient and wait for the right dog to be offered, and then to make searching enquiries about the reason for sale.

The vast majority of potential gundog owners are nevertheless likely to decide on a young puppy from proved working parents, as they are available in far greater numbers and can be brought up from the outset as one of the family. However, a decision then has to be taken as to whether to buy a dog or a bitch. At one time everyone seemed to want dogs, to the extent that dog puppies were usually more expensive to buy than bitches. These days the situation is precisely the opposite, and anyone who still advertises his dog pups at a higher price than his bitches is very much out of touch!

For the one-dog owner, however, there is a great deal to be said for buying a male. The fact that a male cannot give birth to a litter of unwanted puppies ought not to be a factor, as no properly cared-for dog of either sex should be allowed to wander about on its own and therefore this problem should never arise. It must be remembered, though, that a bitch may well choose to come in season at just the time when her owner has booked a week's holiday to go grouse shooting, or for the most important pheasant shoot of the year. Field trialling bitches always seem to come in season at the wrong time, and most experienced gundog owners are still distrustful of the 'pill' which postpones a bitch's heat. Too often there seem to be repercussions in the form of abnormality in subsequent heats. Dogs tend to be just that bit bigger and stronger, and are often slightly tougher in temperament, which may or may not be an advantage.

Bitches are generally accepted to be quieter, gentler, more loyal and easier to train. Their disadvantages have already been pointed out. Experienced trainers vary as to which they prefer, with perhaps the majority favouring bitches. One occasionally comes across a particularly quiet, gentle and affectionate dog, in fact a dog with a bitch's temperament.

14

One of these is perhaps the perfect answer, if he can be found.

An over-sexed dog is an absolute menace on a shooting day where there are other dogs and bitches present. He tends to be quarrelsome with the former and over-amorous with the latter. If he is not careful, the owner of such a pest is likely to find himself notorious in consquence and people finish up by disliking the pair of them equally! The same applies to bad-tempered dogs, which are completely untypical of any of the gundog breeds and no owner should inflict one on his shooting companions.

It is impossible to tell whether a young puppy is going to turn out to be over-sexed or not. Unfortunately the accepted system of breeding, whereby most bitches are sent to famous and popular stud dogs, tends to encourage the production of highly sexed animals, as any dog at public stud must be keen enough to mate any and every bitch put in front of him, whether willing or not.

For dogs which are more interested in bitches than in work, castration, although seeming rather drastic, is well worth considering. Dogs are the only domestic animals which are not neutered almost as a matter of course, and with a male animal it is a very small operation. However, both sexes should be fully mature before neutering is contemplated and a great deal of thought should be given before it is carried out, as once done it cannot be undone.

Bitches are often spayed more for the owner's convenience than for any advantage to the bitch, and I cannot help wondering about the morality of subjecting a healthy animal to a major abdominal operation purely for such a reason. Again, the pros and cons must be thoroughly weighed up before a decision is made. Bitches which are neutered in middle or old age, because of uterine infection or growths, often seem to take on a new lease of life, but young bitches in perfect health are a different matter. In any case, neutered dogs and bitches often have a tendency to put on weight so their diets must be strictly controlled to prevent this.

15

The buyer of a young puppy must resign himself to a long wait before he can get down to any serious training, and an even longer one before the youngster will be of any real use in the shooting field. Most retrievers will be at least eighteen months old before their dummy training is complete, and then a lot of experience in the field is needed before they can be relied on to make much contribution towards the bag.

2 Choosing a Breed

There are five breeds of retriever recognised in Britain by the Kennel Club. In order of popularity these are the Labrador, Golden, Flatcoated, Curly-coated and Chesapeake Bay. The last-named is an American variety specialising in water work. It looks like a large, rangily-built Labrador with a rough coat, and comes in various shades of brown. There are very few in Britain, where for the purposes of choosing a promising puppy from proved working parents the breed can probably be discounted.

Curly-coated Retrievers are a British breed which has fallen somewhat out of fashion. They are fairly large and powerfully built, and their coats, which can be black or liver, consist of tight curls like astrakhan. Formerly they were very popular with keepers as combined gun and guard dogs, but nowadays very few are being worked and virtually none run in trials. It would therefore be difficult for a potential buyer to know where to go to acquire a working-bred puppy, though no doubt a few do still exist.

Flatcoated Retrievers, while being a minority breed in comparison with Labradors and Goldens, have many keen adherents who work them and run them in trials. They are either black or liver, the former being the more common. The secretary of the Flatcoated Retriever Society for the past fifteen years, the Hon Mrs Amelia Jessel, finds them easy to train and has had considerable success with them in field trials. She finds them particularly useful on a grouse moor as, having a substantial proportion of setter blood in their original makeup, they tend to range widely. They have

17

excellent noses and can wind game from a long distance. Alternatively, some Flatcoats will hunt close like a spaniel. Mrs Jessel has never had one which was not keen on dummy work, very important for ease of training, or one which was any real trouble to train to go into water. She also finds them very good in cover. They have a reputation for being slower to mature and possibly more headstrong than other retriever breeds, but Mrs Jessel does not necessarily agree with this.

Mr Eric Baldwin has made four Golden and one Labrador Field Trial Champion, and has also trained Flatcoats and won an Any Variety Non-Winner stake with one. He does find them rather slower to mature than the other two breeds, but loves them for their amusing and clownish characters and a special charm which their owners find they possess. They are highly affectionate, but some can be headstrong and inclined to play up during training.

A young Flatcoat is sufficiently athletic to catch a hare and, if he is ever allowed to do so, it is extremely difficult to prevent him from coursing them for ever afterwards. A Flatcoat's instinct is to range, rather than to hunt close, so in a field trial his handler is often in difficulties keeping him in the area if he does not find his bird quickly. On the other hand, they sometimes win trials on a bad scenting day by virtue of their superior noses.

Mr F. Clitheroe has won the Retriever Championship twice and trained one Golden and four Labrador Field Trial Champions, and has also won the Flatcoated Retriever Open Stake. He considers that Flatcoats are gamefinders second to none, but they tend to work more for themselves than for their handlers. He finds that they have great style and courage but hate interference.

Flatcoats were the universal retrieving dog years ago, before there were many Labradors about or Goldens arrived on the scene. Their fall from popularity in favour of the ubiquitous Labrador seems to have been due to the latter's greater speed and style in hunting and to his biddability, and possibly to his

Plate 1   A Flatcoated Retriever owned by the Hon Mrs Amelia Jessel

smaller size and shorter coat. Mrs Jessel, however, believes that the long coat of the Golden or Flatcoat has certain advantages in protecting its owner from barbed wire injuries, which are common with Labradors.

Mrs J. R. Atkinson is certainly the leading authority on working Golden Retrievers, having made up ten Field Trial Champions herself and bred five more. She has won the Retriever Championship and been second twice, and the vast majority of top trialling Goldens of today have her Holway breeding behind them. She is of the opinion, which seems to be a universal one, that Goldens on the whole are more sensitive than Labradors and more easily upset. It is fatal to lose one's temper with a Golden. They have excellent noses and, like Flatcoats, tend to come into their own at trials on a bad scenting day. Their hunting style is different from that of a Labrador, in that they hunt with heads held high, using the wind rather than ground scent. For this reason some field trial judges tend to treat them unfairly, thinking that if their heads

19

are not down they are not working.

Many Golden owners find that they can use their dogs for beating more successfully than other retriever breeds. Apparently there is less difficulty with them in reconciling the need for close hunting while beating, and wider ranging when seeking unmarked shot birds. It seems that as a breed they mature more slowly than Labradors, although perhaps quicker than Flatcoats. Many Labrador trainers are doing things with their pups at nine months which a Golden owner would not dream of doing at less than a year or even eighteen months.

Mr E. Baldwin's experience with the three breeds has left him with a slight preference for a Golden, though he stresses that they are a sensitive breed and need a quiet, kind trainer. The best Goldens can compete with the best Labradors and even beat them, although it is indisputable that there are more good Labradors about than good Goldens or Flatcoats.

Mr Clitheroe agrees that a good Golden is equal to any Labrador, but takes longer to train. One is likely to be six

Plate 2 Mr Eric Baldwin with the three retriever breeds he owns and trains

Plate 3   Mr E. Baldwin enjoying the company of two Goldens

Plate 4   Mr Dick Male with four Labradors

months behind with a Golden in comparison with a Labrador.

The majority of new owners are likely to decide on a Labrador, as there are more of them to choose from; they are smaller and more compact than the other breeds and thus fit into the house and car more easily, and their short coats are easier to dry and do not smell as strongly as a longer-coated dog does when wet. There is a choice of three colours: black, yellow (never golden) and liver.

Mr R. Male, who trains the Berrystead gundogs for Mr W. C. Williams, OBE, DL, and has made seven Labrador Field Trial Champions, is acknowledged to be a trainer second to none and has handled all three of the main retriever breeds. He is a convinced Labrador enthusiast. He finds them easier to train and generally more co-operative than the others, although he points out that there are some very good Goldens about these days.

Mr A. Wylie has had a lifetime in gundogs, starting in 1914 picking up on a grouse moor with dogs owned by his father, when the latter was otherwise engaged with the Cameron Highlanders. He, too, prefers a Labrador, if only for the reason that on muddy ground it is easier to keep clean. He agrees that Goldens are on the whole milder, more sensitive and easier to control than Labradors, although headstrong ones do exist.

Mr E. Baldwin admits that he can train three Labradors in the time it takes to train two Goldens or one Flatcoat, but stresses that this is purely on the grounds of the time it takes each breed to mature, and is not to be taken as a measure of intelligence.

Mr R. G. Baldwin, however, who has won the Retriever Championship three times and at one period had four Field Trial Champions in his kennels at once, likes a hard dog so he infinitely prefers Labradors to Goldens. He trains the Sendhurst dogs for Mr R. S. Wilkins, and will not tolerate the small, whippety Labradors favoured by some modern field triallists. His kennels are full of good-looking, thoroughly typical dogs which are a joy to the eye of anyone who appreciates the rugged charm of the true Labrador.

Whatever any of the experts say, each individual will choose the dog which attracts him or her most and this is perfectly correct. He is far more likely to make a success of a dog which he has chosen himself than one which he has been persuaded to choose against his better judgement. Flatcoats and Goldens are, to many eyes, more attractive in appearance than Labradors, and this will add greatly to the joy of ownership to the people concerned. It seems to be generally agreed that training methods should be similar for all breeds, although the age to start may vary.

3 Buying a Puppy

Having decided upon the breed and sex, the next problem is to find the right puppy. There are plenty about, especially in the commoner breeds, but there are vast differences between one puppy and another. Different strains within the same breed can vary as much as, or even more than, different breeds, so it is vitally important to select a puppy from a suitable strain according to one's ultimate goal. Hereditary and environmental factors decide the potential of any animal, as they do of human beings. It is therefore necessary to have some idea of what a dog's pedigree can tell you and some way of deciding, if the breeding is right, whether the puppy has been properly reared to realise its full potential both mentally and physically.

A great many people feel baffled if presented with a pedigree, but it is basically quite simple. Parents appear in the left-hand column, grandparents in the next column to the right, and so on. The male parent always appears above the female and is mentioned first when telling someone what a dog's sire and dam are. It is usual to say a dog is 'by' so-and-so (meaning the sire) and 'out of' or 'ex' (meaning the dam).

The nearer relations are likely to have much more influence than remoter ancestors, so less notice need be taken of names appearing far back. It is an accepted fact among breeders that the dam has more influence on her pups than the sire, so it is necessary to make sure that the mother of the litter is satisfactory in every way. It is not enough that the sire may be the leading Field Trial Champion of the day.

Many students of breeding would go so far as to say that the tail-female line, ie the bottom line on the pedigree, is the one of paramount importance. Good bitches are very rarely mated to poor dogs, but the converse frequently happens.

Some breeders add information to their pedigrees, such as 'litter sister to F.T.Ch. So and So'. If not overdone, this can be helpful. Many abbreviations in common use may mean nothing to an inexperienced buyer. Some of these are as follows:

F.T.Ch. (Field Trial Champion). This is the most important one to look for in a working pedigree, as it denotes a dog of outstanding ability.

Ch. (Champion) indicates a show bench champion which has passed a very simple test at a field trial, but does not guarantee anything like the working standard of even a certificate of merit won in actual competition. In fact it means little more than that the dog would retrieve and was not gun shy. It should also mean that he proved himself not hard mouthed, but it is rare for a dog to be asked to retrieve a runner for a qualifier, and many dogs will nip a live bird but not a dead one.

Int. Ch. (International Champion) refers to a dog which has qualified for his title in more than one country.

Sh. Ch. (Show Champion) indicates a show bench champion which has not qualified in the field. More than the odd one or two of these in the pedigree should be regarded with grave suspicion, and certainly it would be inadvisable to buy for work a puppy with a show champion as either sire or dam. However, there are some dogs which have proved both good workers themselves and producers of such, owning a show champion somewhere in their pedigrees.

Dual Ch. (Dual Champion) means a dog which is both a field trial and show champion. No retriever has achieved this for many years, so any dual champions will be well back in the pedigree and can have very little influence.

F.T.W. (Field Trial Winner) is not an official title and in practice is virtually meaningless. If it could be taken to mean what it says, ie that the dog in question had won a field trial, it could be useful, except that different grades of trial vary greatly in standards. Unfortunately some less than scrupulous breeders have used it to indicate a dog which has had any trial award, including a certificate of merit. As it is not officially recognised, it should not be used as a title on any pedigree, though it is perfectly in order and most helpful to see in brackets after a dog's name 'Open Stake Winner' or '10 Field Trial Awards'.

C.O.M. Certificate of Merit (in a field trial). The object of a certificate is to recognise the fact that a dog has run a good trial, committed no major crimes and proved himself to be a thoroughly useful shooting dog. However, standards vary, and not all judges use the same criteria in awarding certificates. A dog which had won several would certainly have proved himself to be a very competent gundog, but if he has nothing more than one certificate, a high standard of ability is not necessarily implied. A certificate in an open stake is likely to mean more than one in a lesser event.

Winner Ret. Ch. (Winner of the Retriever Championship). This is a trial held annually for the top twenty or thirty winning field trial retrievers of the year, of all breeds. Thus the winner in any year is generally accepted to have proved himself to be the outstanding dog of that year. If one or more Retriever Championship winners appear in the first two or three generations of the pedigree, it is very impressive, but I repeat that the dam of the litter must have virtues of her own to contribute. A poor bitch cannot produce good offspring from even the most brilliant sire. Of course, not all Retriever Championship winners are dogs, so a puppy from a Championship-winning bitch would be even more valuable and correspondingly difficult to obtain.

W.T.Ch. (Working Trial Champion). This is an official title won by a few Labradors, along with Alsatians and other breeds usually associated with police and obedience work. The only relevance it has to selecting a gundog is that working trial qualifications (listed below in descending order of importance) show that the dog concerned is at least highly trainable and has a good nose.

P.D.Ex. Police Dog (Excellent). Apart from having to pass a stiff test of tracking, searching, jumping and obedience, a dog with this qualification has had to do police patrol work, including defence of his handler, arresting a running criminal, etc.

T.D.Ex. Tracking Dog (Excellent). This is an alternative open stake qualification to the above, and generally considered to be more suitable for the gundog breeds, as the emphasis is on nosework. The track, which is ordinary human foot scent without any artificial additions, must be at least three hours old and at least half a mile long. Obedience and jumping are included, but not police work.

W.D.Ex. Working Dog (Excellent). As above, except that the track is one and a half hours cold.

U.D.Ex. Utility Dog (Excellent). As above, with a half-hour cold track.

C.D.Ex. Companion Dog (Excellent). There is no track in this, the most junior stake. It consists of a search for one small article, various obedience exercises and the jumps. For all stakes these consist of a 6ft scale, which the dog has to negotiate both ways, a 9ft long jump and a 3ft clear jump, both of which the dog has to clear once without touching.

To be awarded 'Excellent' in any stake the dog has to obtain 80 per cent marks overall and not to fail in any section.

Ob. Ch. or Obed. Ch. (Obedience Champion). This title has been won by a very few Goldens and Labradors. It indicates a high degree of trainability, but not necessarily of the sort which is suitable for gundog training. A very keen, rather excitable temperament tends to be the most success-ful for advanced obedience training, otherwise the degree of precision required soon bores most gundogs.

H.D. free (or similar). This should mean that the dog has

passed the official Kennel Club/British Veterinary Association test for hip dysplasia, but unless the letters 'KC/BVA' appear it is more likely to mean that the breeder's vet has given his opinion that the dog is not actually a serious case of H.D. An explanation should always be asked of any vague term.

H.D. Breeder's Letter. This is the next best thing to a KC/BVA pass certificate. The dog's hips can be faulted, but only to a very minor degree.

P.R.A. free (or similar). Here again, an official KC/BVA scheme exists which is the only meaningful one, as there are only a small number of vets in the country qualified to diagnose Progressive Retinal Atrophy. A responsible breeder will have all breeding stock tested under the scheme and at least the parents and grandparents of the prospective puppy should have been tested. There are different ages in the various retriever breeds for the awarding of a permanent certificate of clinical (not necessarily genetical) freedom from the condition, ranging from four years in Labradors to six years in Goldens. It should be safe to buy a puppy from parents who have only interim certificates, so long as *their* parents have, or had, permanent ones.

Hereditary cataract is also a problem in some breeds, and absence of the condition can be tested for in the same way as P.R.A.

Working test winner. Working tests are unofficial gundog tests run on dummies or cold game. Wins in these are better than nothing, but do not indicate anything about a dog's mouth or behaviour under actual shooting field conditions.

A pup with a pedigree containing champions or show champions need not be rejected if there is also plenty of working stock, with field trial awards, in the immediate ancestry. Although not every gundog owner is interested in field trials, they are the only way in which an owner can prove the working abilities of his stock. Admittedly there are some perfectly good working dogs whose owners never run them in trials, but in such cases the prospective buyer would be wise to see the parents of his pup actually out in the shooting field before committing himself.

Plate 5   Mrs Audrey Radclyffe and some of her yellow Labradors

In all breeds of retriever there are some breeders who are trying to combine good looks with working ability, and are succeeding in doing so. A notable example in Labradors is Mrs A. M. Radclyffe, whose kennel of dual-purpose yellows was founded in 1929. She has produced from the same strain one Champion and four Field Trial Champions, plus a great many other winners in both spheres, including several Field Trial Champions made up by other people. She herself has twice won second in the Retriever Championship.

The buyer who is seeking a good-looking working puppy should choose a breeder with successes in both spheres, but whose main interest is on the working side. This should immediately be apparent by the proportion of working to show successes their dogs have achieved. Those not concerned with their dogs' appearance can go with an easy mind to a breeder with similar views. However, it is worth considering that a gundog is actually working for only a small proportion of his life. For the rest of it his owner has to look at him, so it will be all to the good if his appearance gives pleasure.

If both parents are reasonably handsome, there is a fair chance of the pups being handsome too if they are properly reared. Most breeders are glad to help in picking the pup with the desired potential. The purchaser should be entirely frank, and if he has a particular dislike of a certain fault, such as light eyes or a curly tail, should say so. It will be too late when the pup which has become a loved member of the family suddenly starts carrying his tail over his back or develops a piercing yellow gaze reminiscent of foglamps!

Hereditary diseases also present problems. The main ones, mentioned earlier, are P.R.A. and H.D., but there are also others, such as entropion, epilepsy, pancreatic deficiency and tendency to heart disease. One must retain a sense of proportion, but it is as well to be aware of these things. The breeder should be able virtually to guarantee freedom from P.R.A. and hereditary cataract, and should at least be aware of the existence of H.D. and have X-rayed his breeding stock. The KC/BVA scheme only recognises perfection with a pass certificate, or near-perfection with a 'Breeder's Letter'. There are plenty of dogs with perfectly functional hips which are not good enough to be certified under the scheme. The individual must decide how much importance to attach to H.D. certificates; these after all only guarantee clinical freedom from the condition, which the dog may still be genetically capable of passing on to his progeny. He must also decide how far to trust the breeder who states that his vet assures him his bitch's hips are all right. The same applies to such things as epilepsy. A breeder who says there are no known cases in his line should be believed if the buyer has done his homework properly and a reputable breeder has been chosen.

Entropion is unique among hereditary diseases in that it can be cured by operation. It is therefore not so much of a disaster if a pup turns out to have it, so long as there is no desire to breed from him or her. For humane reasons, any dog suffering from entropion *must* be operated on, as the condition consists of in-turned eyelids, causing the lashes constantly to irritate the eyeball. It does not take much imagination to realise how agonising this must be. A conscientious person would never breed from a case of entropion, and re-mate most warily, and to different partners, parents which had produced it. If there is the slightest chance of entropion in the line, it is vital to watch for any sign of runny eyes in the pups, though often the condition does not manifest itself until the dog is several months old. It would have to be a very bad case to be apparent by seven or eight weeks.

Some people advocate fighting shy of inbreeding. The ignorant will also talk about a dog being 'too highly bred', whatever that might be intended to mean, for it does not in fact mean anything. Inbreeding means the mating together of close relations—ie father to daughter, son to mother, or brother to sister. Anything else, such as grandfather to grand-daughter or half-brother to half-sister, is called line-breeding, and is practised to a greater or lesser degree by *all* successful breeders in *all* forms of livestock. If one name appears many times in a pedigree, questions should be asked, including a straight one as to why the breeder has chosen to line-breed so closely to that particular dog. The usual answer will be that he was an outstandingly good one, which is fine so long as he does not also throw some undesirable recessive fault. It is probably safer to choose a puppy from a litter not too closely line-bred, and for this reason it is essential to see at least a four-generation pedigree. However, it must be remembered that inbreeding and line-breeding *produce* nothing, either good or bad. They merely intensify what is already there. That is why all breeders line-breed to some extent as soon as they are achieving something approaching what they are aiming for.

Out-crossing means the mating together of totally unrelated stock. In fact this is a near impossibility, as all well-bred dogs of any breed originally come from comparatively few ancestors.

Inter-breeding is *not* another word for inbreeding. It used to mean the mating of two dogs of different varieties of the same breed—for example, a Golden to a Labrador, or a Springer to a Cocker. The term is now obsolete in gundogs as what were formerly merely varieties have been reclassified as distinct breeds. The product of the matings cited would now therefore rank as crossbreeds, which are the product of two pure-bred dogs of different breeds. A mongrel is a complete hotch-potch of breeds, and therefore outside the range of this book.

A puppy should ideally be booked well in advance. The right sort of breeder will probably have a waiting list, especially for bitch puppies. It is desirable to see the prospective dam, and the sire too if he lives within reach, before coming to a decision. If a breeder can show the dam, possibly her dam, and young adults from a similar mating to the one proposed, and they are all of the type and temperament sought, the choice is probably as safe as anything can be in the world of livestock. The breeder should be happy to show all his dogs, by appointment, and give a short demonstration, if only on dummies. The dogs should be friendly, although it is perfectly natural that they should bark until their owner appears. They should not, however, bite, if they have the correct retriever temperaments! If an owner appears unwilling to let his dogs out of the kennel, suspect their temperaments. He may say that he is afraid of infection and this could be genuine, but temperament is too important a matter to be left in doubt. A friendly temperament is absolutely essential for a gundog which, when he is trained, will be expected to mix with strange dogs and pile into crowded vehicles, and will be approached and petted on a shooting day by a number of strangers, who do not expect a retriever to be anything but calm and good-tempered.

Thought should be given to the best time of year to acquire a puppy. The owner of a genuine working bitch will be most unlikely to want her out of action during the shooting season, so pups of this sort are likely to be available for sale only from about May to October. A pup born in March, April or May will have summer weather in which to do his main growing, will be ready for training the following spring and summer, and able to start work in the autumn or winter. Spring and early summer are the times when the majority of working puppies are bred, as most owners mate their bitches during their first heat after the end of the shooting season, or in January, as a bitch can work until she is five or six weeks in whelp.

There is much to be said for buying two puppies instead of one. If the puppy is to be kennelled, rather than live in the house, the company of another dog is almost essential. Mrs D. Purbrick, who has kept and trained Labradors for around half a century, during which time she has made up six Field Trial Champions, would go so far as to say that, unless the new owner is prepared to buy two puppies, he should leave his choice with the breeder until it is five or six months old. Her theory is that a puppy removed from the litter at seven or eight weeks and brought up in human company hardly realises that it is a dog. However, not everyone brings up their puppies as well as Mrs Purbrick does, with plenty of the right sort of food and the run of a huge grass enclosure alongside the road, thus accustoming the youngsters to noise, people and traffic. Equally, not many breeders would be prepared to run on puppies for other people for more than a few weeks.

Buying two puppies reduces the odds against success, though it may later be necessary to harden one's heart and sell one of them. The part-trained or trained reject, if he has no serious faults and is well bred, should be worth more than he has cost to rear because of the scarcity on the market of older puppies. Two pups will exercise and amuse each other to some extent, although they will do more than twice the damage of one puppy. It is very difficult to house-train two puppies together, because if a mistake is made it can seldom be known which one made it.

Likely breeders may be found by asking among knowledgeable gundog-owning friends, or by studying advertisements in the sporting press. If there is no hurry, the latter method should be satisfactory, provided that the checks suggested earlier are carried out. Some may feel that they are more likely to get an honest deal from a small-time amateur than an established breeder, but this is not the case, as the latter has a valuable reputation to maintain and the former probably has not. However, there is no harm at all in buying a puppy from a friend having a once-and-for-all litter from his precious only bitch in order to breed a pup for himself, so long as the person concerned has taken the trouble to find out something about the pitfalls of breeding, particularly as regards hereditary diseases, and how the puppies should be reared.

Certainly a one-off litter usually comes in for a lot of petting and attention, which is an excellent thing; in fact it is absolutely essential for the future mental health of the dog that he should have had prolonged 'humanisation' from the age of three weeks. This does not mean just visiting the puppies at feeding time, but spending a great deal of time playing with them, studying their developing characters, and even giving them a little elementary training, such as coming when they are called and retrieving a small, soft dummy from a few yards distance. Until about five weeks, puppies' eyes cannot focus properly, so they will not see anything thrown more than a foot or two in front of them. However, there is no reason why an eight-week-old pup should not be retrieving happily to hand, and be impervious to the noise of a starting pistol fired at a little distance. It is up to the modern breeder to accustom his pups to various sorts of noise, as they are bound to have to endure it in some form or other, even in the depths of the country. If the breeder is seen to have used some imagination, such as putting a radio in the kennel, to overcome this problem, it is probable that he has been careful and thoughtful in other ways too.

Once chosen, the breeder should be trusted. He will be able to advise on which puppy to pick, according to the temperament required. It cannot be too strongly emphasised that different temperaments suit different owners, and this applies just as much to the experts as to anyone else. Mr Bob Baldwin likes a really tough, hard dog and succeeds brilliantly with this type, whereas Mr Eric Baldwin, Mr Clitheroe and others like the soft, easier type and find they get their best results from them. The proportion of trainers liking soft as opposed to hard dogs seems to be at least three or four to one, so if after due consideration the new buyer is still unsure of what type he should go for, it might be wiser to assume that he is likely to be in the majority. Certainly that sort of dog, once trained, is far easier to keep disciplined. A soft dog should not, however, be confused with a nervous one. The latter would be a difficult proposition for most people to cope with, as so much time would have to be spent trying to build up confidence before anything much in the way of training could be achieved.

The breeder will know the temperaments of the parents and thus be in a position to advise on whether to pick the most lively pup or one of the quieter ones. It is possible that the pup which is usually the live wire of the litter is for some reason feeling a little off-colour on the day the buyer arrives to make a choice, possibly opening the way to a wrong decision unless the breeder is enlisted to help.

Most experienced trainers have their pet theories about picking puppies. Mrs Purbrick advises choosing the puppy which comes up to the buyer, as it is thus indicating that it has chosen him! She also suggests making a point of falling over a bucket or contriving some other loud noise, and choosing the puppy that comes to see what the commotion is about.

It is almost universally recommended to choose the puppy

which sits and looks at one intelligently, and not necessarily the boldest. Mr Clitheroe also looks for a hard-wagging tail, indicating a potentially stylish worker.

Mr Eric Baldwin attaches a great deal of importance to choosing his puppies. First he studies the breeding very carefully, then asks the breeder to leave him alone with the litter for anything up to an hour. He puts away the ones of the wrong sex, or any whose looks he does not like for any reason. He then sees if the remaining pups individually will retrieve, or at least pick something up, and will keep running up to him. If there are two of apparently equal temperament he picks the best looking, going for a good head, short back and correct tail carriage.

Unless several visits are feasible, the puppies should not be inspected before they are seven weeks old. At this age they should all come boldly up, tails wagging. They should have seen plenty of strangers of both sexes and have learnt that there is nothing to fear from them.

Physically, the puppy should be strong boned, fairly plump, bright-eyed, and well grown. This, of course, will be difficult to judge for those not used to looking at puppies, but as a very rough guide an eight-week-old Labrador should weigh about 14-16lb. If the parents are small, and a small dog is wanted, it will not matter if they are less than that, provided they look well nourished. The size of the pups' feet and ears often gives some indication of how big they are going to grow. I have had puppies weighing nearly 20lb at eight weeks, when there have been only two or three in the litter, and it has been impossible to stop them making enormous growth in the early weeks. They do not, however, finish any bigger than normal as adults. Huge puppies are said to be more susceptible to hip dysplasia, so great size at an early age is no particular virtue.

The puppies' coats should appear clean and healthy, their ears should not be waxy and their toenails should be short. This latter point is an indication of the sort of care they have had. A breeder who neglects to cut nails when necessary is probably neglectful in other ways. The kennel and run should be clean. If asked how often he mucks out, the breeder should not answer 'once a day' or 'twice a day', but 'whenever I go into the kennel'. Assuming the pups are being fed four times daily, as they should be at that age, they are likely to be visited by a conscientious owner at least five or six times a day. Any droppings which may have escaped attention should be firm rather than loose, and medium or dark in colour.

The pups should certainly not be scratching. Fleas and lice, especially the latter, are common on long-haired dogs and precautions against them should have been taken by the breeder.

Virtually all pups are born with roundworms, which they get from the bloodstream of the dam (it makes no difference if she has been wormed), but they should be clear of them by selling age, having been wormed at least twice. It is possible with modern remedies to worm puppies from three weeks of age, so there is no excuse for not having done so. The pups should not be infected with tapeworms, but there is a distinct danger that they may be if they have fleas, as the flea is an intermediate host of the tapeworm. Dogs acquire tapeworms either by swallowing fleas or by eating infected rabbit or sheep droppings.

There is a characteristic, unique and rather pleasant 'puppy smell' which pups lose soon after about eight weeks. Certainly no puppy should smell in any way unpleasant, and neither should the kennel in which he is housed. The kennel should incorporate a warm, dry and cosy bed and a roomy run for the puppies to play in.

No puppy should be collected before eight weeks old, or certainly seven weeks. Anyone trying to part with a puppy younger is more interested in his profit margin than in the welfare of his stock. Apart from anything else, there is no reason why the dam, if properly and generously fed, should not still occasionally be feeding her litter right up to eight or nine weeks, although they should be in no way dependent on her for food at that age. Mother's milk is the finest possible food for a puppy, and also contains valuable antibodies to protect the pup against disease. That is why most vets will not inoculate pups until they are about twelve weeks and the antibodies obtained from the mother's milk have passed out of the body.

If it is not convenient to collect the pup until after he is eight weeks old, the breeder is perfectly entitled to charge the buyer for his keep after that time.

If the prospective buyer has not had the opportunity of making a prior visit to the kennels to see the adult dogs and to make as certain as possible that the puppies are going to be the type he wants, he should make a firm resolution to be as hard-headed as possible about coming to a sensible decision. It is very easy to be carried away by the charm which all young animals possess, and to go home with a particular pup even though one's better judgement advises against it. Spouses and children too can often make a sensible decision even more difficult, by falling in love with what is patently the wrong puppy.

On the other hand, I personally will never sell a puppy to a man unless I know that his wife (or mother or housekeeper or whoever) wants it as much as he does. Whoever in theory owns the dog, it is upon the housewife that all the early chores of feeding, mopping up, etc, devolve! Do not be surprised if the breeder asks some pointed questions, as he (or she, as some women make very successful dog breeders) should be extremely concerned about the sort of homes the pups are going to.

If all these points are as they should be, do not expect to be able to buy the puppy for less than the cost of producing it—which, amazingly, a lot of people do seem to expect. It is very hard for a breeder to show a profit on a litter of puppies. Not only is the cost of the right sort of food very high, but vet's fees, advertising, Kennel Club documentation, postage, telephoning, bedding, disinfectant, worm medicines etc, all have to be considered and the cost of them is going up all the time. Not only that, if the parents have been successful in competition, their owner will have spent heavily in travelling to trials all over the country. His name and reputation are worth something. Few breeders ever add up the labour costs of rearing a litter. They dare not. Hours of every day are taken up, not only with caring for the puppies, but in answering enquiries for them, writing out pedigrees and dealing with visitors. Naturally the owner of an unknown bitch is likely to charge less, and may offer a good bargain if the dam is well bred, the sire was carefully chosen and the litter well reared. However, he cannot provide the expert advice and after-sales service which an established breeder will give, without stint, both at the time of sale and for the rest of the dog's life.

The breeder should supply, along with pedigree, registration certificate, etc, a diet sheet. If the puppy is being fed on a particular proprietary brand of dog food, he should offer the buyer a supply, so as not to risk upsetting the pup by a sudden change of diet.

4 Early Upbringing (Playgroup Stage)

A retriever puppy at birth weighs about 1lb and in one year may have grown to something like 65lb. It is therefore evident that plenty of good food will be needed to accomplish this tremendous growth rate without the puppy becoming leggy and weedy. He should be on four meals a day at eight weeks, spread out as evenly as possible from first thing in the morning to last thing at night, and consisting basically of two meat and two milk meals. At three months the number of meals can be reduced to three, and at six months or so to two. Quantities will depend upon the breed, sex and individual growth rate, but as a rough guide a retriever puppy will eat ½oz meat per day for every pound of its weight, or 1oz for every week of its life, until a maximum of about 1½lb daily has been reached. If one of the complete dry foods is being used, however, the amount of meat required will be less than this. Plenty of milk should be included in the diet as long as the puppy is still growing, and one of the calcium and Vitamin D products is also desirable for optimum growth of bones and teeth. The aim should be to keep a puppy just nicely covered, but not too fat. Fresh water should, of course, always be available.

It should have been decided before bringing the puppy home whether or not he is to live in the house. There is no reason why he should not be perfectly happy as a kennel dog all his life, provided he has other canine company and has plenty of outings and exercise, and the kennel is dry and cosy and not in too isolated a position. The ideal is a draughtproof insulated brick or wooden building, plus a good-sized run which should be at least partly concreted and on a slight slope so that puddles do not collect. It should contain a closed-in bed big enough for the dog to stretch out in, but not so big that he cannot warm it with his own body heat. Wheat straw, wood wool or newspaper are all suitable forms of bedding, and care should be taken that it is always dry and clean.

Plate 6   F.T.Ch. Hedenhampark Holcot Fay and Mr Frank Clitheroe's
children demonstrate that top trial dogs can also be family pets

Opinions among the top trainers are divided about the desirability of keeping potential gundogs in the house. Most agree that it does no harm so long as the puppy is sensibly treated, and taken out rather than let out. Mr Clitheroe lets his children play with the dogs and puppies, but has a strict rule that there is to be no retrieving in any shape or form.

Mrs Purbrick and Mrs Radclyffe disapprove of puppies undergoing training being kept in the house at all, but Mr

Wylie thinks it is an excellent thing and points out that a considerable amount of preliminary training with a young puppy can take place indoors. The pup can be taught to sit and to retrieve a dummy, and the more he is with his trainer the more he comes to understand what is said to him.

Most people, especially if they have only one dog, prefer to keep it in the house. There is no reason why a gundog should not be a house pet, so long as he is treated with intelligence and consideration by all members of the household. It is necessary to have somewhere where he can be shut up when occasion demands, so a kennel and run of some sort is almost essential. If the owner is out for a long time it is unkind to leave a house-trained dog shut in the house.

When the new puppy arrives home, it is very unwise to allow him the run of the house straight away. House training is based on the primitive instinct to keep the den clean, and it cannot be expected that a small puppy should think of an entire house as his den. Keep him confined to one room at first. Better still, barricade off a corner of the kitchen, utility room or whatever room has the most suitable floor, and cover it with newspaper. At first the puppy should be taken outside every two hours, after every feed, and every time he wakes up after a sleep, and praised for performing in the right place. When someone is free to keep an eye on him he can of course be taken into other rooms, but not allowed to wander about unobserved. The more time that is given to concentrating on a puppy during the first fortnight or so, the quicker he will be house trained. Puppies vary in how long it is before they can last through the night, but if he is confined to within a few feet of his bed it is certain that he will keep the area clean if he possibly can.

It has been suggested that the puppy should not be allowed to wander around the house at first. In fact, it is probably wisest never to allow the dog to do this until he is a mature, trained adult. It will often be noticed that people brought up with animals automatically shut doors and gates behind them.

Others do not! The conscientious owner should always know exactly where his dog is. Dogs are creatures of habit and routine, and will become perfectly resigned to spending the greater part of their time shut either in the kennel or in the part of the house assigned to them, provided that they are taken out often enough to relieve themselves and have a change of scenery. At least the confined dog is not getting into mischief, neither is he being ticked off by non-doggy members of the household for crimes he cannot possibly understand as such—for example, walking on the drawing room carpet with muddy feet.

The first night or two after leaving his brothers and sisters the puppy is bound to be lonely and unhappy. It is probably best to ignore his howls (if one can) as he will eventually tire and go to sleep. However, a large marrow bone to chew, a well-wrapped hot water bottle in his bed, and a loudly ticking clock nearby, will all help. The latter supposedly has a soothing effect on puppies by simulating the maternal heartbeat. If one weakens and takes the puppy up to one's bedroom, a habit is being started which may last the rest of his life!

When the pup has had a few days to settle down, it is possible to start teaching him to walk on a lead. I prefer to use a rope or nylon slip lead rather than a collar and lead, as the former slackens when the pup ceases to pull, and the latter does not. However, a choke chain would be rather too severe for a young puppy. It is a waste of money buying a collar and lead for a puppy, as he will so quickly grow out of them, and a perfectly serviceable lead can be made out of 5 or 6ft of clothes line.

The puppy should be persuaded to follow at the left side, except that a left-handed owner may prefer to train his dog to walk on the right. The chances are that he will follow without realising that he is attached, and may seize hold of the lead and trot along carrying it. This does not matter, as sooner or later he is bound to either dart ahead or lag behind, in which case he will be brought up with a jerk. He is then likely to

Plate 7   The author showing that a young puppy can be taught to walk
happily on a lead

indulge in a fish-on-a-line act, which should be ignored, except to maintain a firm but gentle 'feel' on the lead. When he stops, bend down and coax him to you, after which you should persuade him to follow for a few more feet before releasing him and ending the lesson. He should always be released when he is in the right position, at one's side on a loose lead, neither dragging back nor pulling ahead, and never immediately after a battle, otherwise he might think he had won it. Most puppies of eight to ten weeks learn to walk on the lead very quickly and easily, and some give no trouble at all. When he has learnt the basic principle, he must be taught not to rush from side to side. If he darts in front the temptation to avoid walking into him should be resisted. He will soon learn that if he gets under foot he will be trodden on. If he tries to cross over behind, give him a fairly gentle jerk back into position. The severity of the jerk will depend upon the temperament of the puppy. One needs to create an impression on him, but not to frighten him. Lead-walking sessions with a young puppy should be very short, probably not more than two or three minutes.

The puppy should not be taken about among other dogs until he has finished his inoculations, which most vets like to give at twelve and fourteen weeks. However, he can and should go for short journeys in the car before this. If he was sick on the way home when collected from his breeder, he already has the idea of being car sick in his mind. This must be eradicated. It is quite a good idea to feed him in the stationary car a few times, and then start him very gradually on extremely short journeys, and never directly after a meal. In this way no further trouble may be experienced, especially if it is possible to make him look forward to going in the car by taking him a few miles in it to somewhere where he can be given a good run off the lead. With obstinate cases, however, it may be necessary to resort to travel sickness tablets for a while until the habit of vomiting can be broken.

The dog's travelling position in the car should be decided and adhered to right from the start. This is quite easily accomplished by someone other than the driver pushing the puppy back every time he tries to leave his position.

The importance of plenty of undisturbed sleep to a young puppy cannot be over-emphasised. He should have his own bed in his own quiet corner, and the children should be strictly forbidden to wake him up. Puppies left to play together regulate their own play/sleep cycles, but it should be explained to children that puppies need a great deal more sleep than they do, and games should therefore not continue so long as to exhaust the puppy.

A puppy coming into a household is a bundle of instincts and desires, some of which need to be eradicated and some harnessed to one's own ends. 'Start as you mean to go on' is the best motto, and a small puppy must not be allowed to get away with something for which he is likely to be punished as an adult. That is grossly unfair. If it is decided that the dog is not to be allowed on the furniture, nothing is easier than to stop him getting on it right from the start. It is, of course, very tempting to pick the puppy up and cuddle him, but there is no way of explaining to him that this must cease as soon as he gets to a certain size. I cuddle my puppies a lot, but make a point of sitting on the floor to do it, so as not to confuse them over the idea of that being their place.

The same applies if it is not desired for the dog to come upstairs—he should be prevented from doing so the first time he tries. It should be borne in mind, however, that one day it might be necessary for him to negotiate a flight of steps, say, at a railway station, so going up and down steps somewhere other than in the house should form part of his education.

Jumping up is a most annoying habit in a house dog—if not to his owner, then certainly to visitors. It is impossible to explain to a dog when one has one's best clothes on, so it is far safer to teach him never to jump up. This is not very easy with a small puppy, but even at the earliest stage he should not be allowed to scrabble at one's legs for attention. The technique is to anticipate the puppy's approach by bending down and patting and praising him for having all four feet on the ground. As he grows it becomes progressively easier to knock him off balance with a quick knee in his chest as he jumps up, but it is essential *immediately* to bend down and praise him when his forefeet return to the ground, or the impression might be given that he is not to rush up and greet his handler, which would be disastrous. Always try and anticipate his approach and be ready for him in a stooping position. Once the dog has learnt that standing on his hind legs is wrong, it will be found that he is far less likely to stand up and steal things off the kitchen table.

If the puppy is greeted delightedly every time he approaches, it will follow that he is delighted to come when called. It will only start to occur to him not to come if and when he discovers it pays to disobey. It is up to the owner to make sure that he never makes this discovery. However, the day is bound to come when he has to be called in order to be put on the lead after he has been playing loose, to be shut up, to have his nails cut or something else he may not like. The bad impression should be eradicated by first praising the pup for coming, before doing anything else. Also, the pup should often be called, praised for coming, and then released. The occasional tit-bit can be very useful in this context.

The aim should always be to instil good habits, rather than to have to break bad ones. Dogs have very simple little brains. They are not capable of thinking things out, but are very quick at connecting cause and effect. For instance, if the puppy is called and he comes, and immediately without a word he is shut in his kennel, he has been punished for coming just as surely as if he had been thrashed. Equally, before punishing him for something, it is essential to make absolutely sure that he knows exactly what he has done wrong. If he has chewed the leg of a chair, take him right up to the chair and close his jaws around the piece he has been chewing, whilst administering a severe scolding. Hitting dogs accomplishes nothing except to relieve the owner's feelings. It is not a punishment they understand. A dog is a pack animal, which is why it is unkind to keep one confined with neither human nor canine companionship. In nature he takes his orders from the pack leader, who is either the biggest and strongest member of the pack or the one with the most dominant personality. To have a proper relationship with a dog, it is essential that the owner is accepted by the dog as his pack leader. In fact it can be positively dangerous for this not to be so. Most cases of dogs biting their owners or members of his family arise from the dog having been allowed to think himself the boss. For instance, if a tiny puppy growls at someone approaching when he is chewing a bone, it should be very firmly taken from him, and the puppy severely shaken and scolded if he tries to bite. This is potentially far too serious a situation for half measures. Unless the owner can do what he wishes to the dog without protest, something is radically wrong with their relationship.

Dogs must be handled in such a way as to make the most of their differing temperaments. With a dog of dominant personality—in other words, a pack leader type—it is necessary to be far more assertive than with a submissive type. The pack leader will punish a recalcitrant member of the pack by a show of strength. That is why it is so very effective in subduing a dog to pick him up with one hand each side of his neck and shake him. It would be a very strong pack leader who could do that! Equally, to hold the dog down with his head on the floor, scolding gruffly, has a similar effect. A docile, submissive dog is rarely if ever likely to need this sort of treatment.

Mrs Purbrick is particularly emphatic on the subject of punishing a dog like a dog—that is to say, by shaking rather than by smacking.

Praise should have a much bigger part to play in dog training than punishment in any form. A dog of good working temperament exists to please its owner, and will do all it can to achieve this. Anything the dog does right should be rewarded with a kind word and/or caress, rather than the purely negative approach of ignoring good behaviour and punishing bad. Many people seem to be too self-conscious to praise their dogs, especially in public. This is a pity, as it means that the dog will never learn to work as happily as he would otherwise do. However, a line must be drawn somewhere, and it is almost as bad to over-praise as to under-praise. A small achievement should be rewarded with a pat and a word. Keep the histrionics for when they are really indicated!

If the relationship with the dog has developed along the right lines, he knows when one is pleased with him and when one is not, without a constant running commentary, to which a dog will eventually close his ears thus making it harder to get through to him when it is really necessary. A quiet tone should always be used. Dogs have very acute hearing, and there is *no* need to shout. A raised voice can therefore be kept in reserve in case of real need.

The timing of praise and correction is all-important. One must be ready immediately to speak or act, otherwise the dog will not make the necessary connection between action and result. It is galling to watch a novice trainer trying to get his dog to retrieve something which it is reluctant to pick up, standing in dead silence while the dog examines the object. If he had said, 'Good dog! Fetch it!' in encouraging tones the second the dog reached the article, and then turned and run away, the chances are that the dog would have seized the object and hurried after his handler, instead of giving the article a good sniffing over and then leaving it.

It seems to be instinctive in some people to time their words and actions correctly, and to ask neither too much nor too little of their dogs in the way of understanding. At any gundog or obedience class one will see some natural handlers, who are bound to succeed, and others who unfortunately never will, beyond a certain point. So much of training is common sense—the least common commodity in the world.

The first thing most people will say when told that one is training a dog is, 'Oh, how patient you must be!' It is certainly helpful to be patient by nature, but not as essential with an intelligent and co-operative dog as it is to have this sense of timing and appreciation of the limitations of the canine mind.

It is vital to be consistent in one's commands and to use the same word always to mean the same thing. 'No' must quickly become an important part of the trainer's vocabulary, and should mean 'Stop what you are doing immediately'. The dog, of course, does not understand the word, only the severe tone of voice in which it is used. Later on, 'No' will also mean 'You must not carry out the action I know you are contemplating!' It is essential to keep one jump ahead of the dog and to know what it is likely to do next. One should also have a word of release, such as 'All right', which means 'Go and do what you like'. This is used to release a dog from the sit position or from walking at heel, etc. 'Sit' must mean 'Sit until I tell you to get up', not 'Sit, but get up again as soon as you feel like it'.

A young retriever puppy is likely to be constantly carrying things, and that is all to the good. It can, however, be irritating to have *everything* retrieved that is left lying around, but unforunately one must either put up with it or learn tidier habits! If one either shouts at the puppy for picking things up or, worse still, snatches them away roughly, one can say goodbye for ever to having a really willing and happy retrieving dog, or one that delivers well. A puppy carrying a stick can safely be ignored, but if it is something more valuable one must call the puppy up, praise him and gently remove the object. Once the puppy is coming when he is called 100 per cent of the time, some elementary retrieving lessons can be given. Use a small soft dummy, glove, or some similar article, but not one of the puppy's own toys. Get the pup's attention and throw the dummy a few yards. He will almost certainly dash to it and pick it up, whereupon one must bend down and encourage him to bring it right up to one. If he hesitates to come, run away. If he still hesitates, lie flat on the ground. Very few puppies can resist this! Do not stare at him

Plate 8   One method of persuading a puppy to bring its retrieve to hand!

50

Plate 9 Mr Bob Baldwin, who is well known for his use of a tennis racket
in training, demonstrates eye contact between dog and handler

as he approaches, but look above or slightly to one side of him. People feel self-conscious walking towards someone who is looking them unwaveringly in the eye, and dogs feel the same. On the other hand, eye contact between handler and dog is important, and anyone who has had a good relationship with a trained dog of any sort will realise that he is in the habit of 'catching the dog's eye' before issuing a command. Some dogs get to the stage of knowing, as soon as eye meets eye, what is wanted, and act accordingly. This sometimes has to be discouraged—for instance, in the case of a dog which one only has to look at for it to run in!

When the puppy has finally brought the article right up to hand, wait a considerable time, praising constantly, before attempting to take the article from his mouth. People are nearly always far too anxious to take the retrieve from the puppy, forgetting that, to him, this will be a mild form of

51

Plate 10 The author giving a young puppy prolonged praise and fondling before attempting to take the retrieve

punishment and will make him far less likely to bring the dummy to hand next time.

Sessions should be kept *very* short. One, two or three retrieves are plenty, but the last should always be a good one. If, however, the pup is not in the mood and things go wrong, it is better to stop on a bad note than to go on and on with a rapidly tiring and bored puppy. If this occurs, several days should elapse before trying again, in the hope that the puppy will have forgotten his previous lack of co-operation.

If a retriever puppy is old enough to have left the nest, he is old enough to retrieve to hand. If he will not pick up the article chosen, try another. It is inconceivable that a properly bred and intelligently chosen retriever puppy will not pick up anything at all! If the difficulty is in getting him to bring the object, try in a confined space so that there is nowhere for the puppy to go except back to his handler. A narrow corridor is ideal.

52

Mrs Radclyffe does all her early retrieving training in a narrow passageway until the habit of retrieving straight to hand is completely established. She estimates that as many as 200 retrieves may be necessary before this point is reached.

Otherwise, one should station oneself between the puppy and his bed or kennel. He will usually try to take the article back there. Intercept him as he tries to pass, but remember to praise, praise and praise again before attempting to take his treasure away. A puppy that *will* not bring his retrieve to hand, when all these methods have been tried, can be cured with the use of a check-cord, but it is essential that he is extremely keen on picking up and carrying, or one runs the risk of putting him off and ending with a far worse problem than that with which one started.

If it is certain that the puppy will not be unduly frightened, the method is to put a light cord 10 or 12ft long on him, holding the other end in one's hand. The dummy should then be thrown within the range of the cord and when the puppy has picked it up, he should be gently restrained from running off with it, and coaxed towards one, pulling gently if necessary. If he drops the dummy, still coax him in, praise him for coming, and throw it again. If he drops it this time, abandon the cord. However, the chances are that he will quickly learn that when the dummy is in his mouth he *must* return with it. Do not stop using the cord too soon, before a habit has been established as, if things go wrong and it is necessary to revert to the cord, the pup may have learnt the difference between having it on and not, in which case the cord will be useless for the rest of the dog's training life. Once the pup has learnt that he has got to bring his retrieve to his handler, willingness, happiness and speed will follow shortly, if praise is unstintingly given.

There is not much point in going on too long with these elementary retrieving lessons. Once the pup is dashing out, picking up the dummy and coming straight back with it, there is no more that can be done until he is taught steadiness, which must come later. It is not a good idea to go on too long letting the puppy get the idea that he may run in to something he sees thrown. A few of the top trainers never let their pupils run in at all. The majority do so at first, however, to encourage marking ability, keenness and speed.

It is just as well not to do any retrieving while the pup is teething, from about three to five months, in case while picking up the dummy he gives a painful jerk to a loose tooth, which could well put him off.

Retriever puppies tend to be terrible chewers. If they chew furniture, walls etc, they can be punished in the way previously described, but it is not worth punishing them for destroying small, portable objects, such as shoes, for fear of giving them inhibitions about retrieving. The only answer is not to leave such things within the puppy's reach. Plenty of harmless things to chew should be provided for as long as the puppy wants them, well into adulthood in some cases, and especially during teething. Large marrow bones will last a long time as they seem to retain their attraction for dogs long after any smell or flavour has left them. Logs of wood with the bark still on are also suitable chewing objects, but not splintery pieces of wood of the kindling type. Intelligent puppies with active brains hate doing nothing except when they are asleep, so at any time when one is not free to supervise and entertain them they should have some suitable toys with which to occupy themselves. Working-bred puppies can in fact be very naughty and extremely trying to have around the house, simply because of the very activity of their brains and their excessive energy.

During all this early growing-up period, owner and pup should spend as much time as possible together, getting to know each other and building up a pleasant and happy relationship. It does not matter all that much who feeds the puppy, but it matters a great deal who takes him out for walks, especially for enjoyable rambles without the lead. Do not over-exercise a young puppy, but from about four months, or after the inoculations have taken effect, it should be possible to take him for half an hour's stroll every day. If there are other dogs in the household, try to take the puppy out by himself sometimes. Otherwise, when the time comes for serious training to commence, it may well be found that the pup is unhappy without the confidence-boosting presence of the other dogs he has come to rely on, and the minute the slightest compulsion is exerted he will run home or back to the car.

Mrs Atkinson has a unique method of bringing up puppies, which she admits goes against what virtually everyone else would recommend. She gives them a tremendous amount of freedom. They are loose all day and are allowed to follow her horse, and to hunt and chase until serious training commences at eight to eleven months, according to the time of year. However, they have to come when they are called before this, and to stop chasing if so ordered. Mrs Atkinson is adamant that if one gives an order it *must* be obeyed, so if it is liable to be ignored it is better not given, and a blind eye turned to whatever the puppy is doing.

When out for walks the pup can be started entering cover by the owner walking through it himself, beginning with light cover such as long grass or dead bracken. The pup should be encouraged to investigate bushes and to go into water, if there is any. Other dogs can be of use in teaching the pup a fondness for cover and water. When he sees that they enjoy them, he will want to join in the fun. A shallow stream which the owner can wade across, persuading the pup to follow, is the best introduction to water.

When out for a walk, either alone or with other dogs, the pup must learn to watch his handler. When his attention wanders and he gets some distance away, try hiding from him. It is amazing how, if one stands still, a pup will fail to see one even when quite close. When one has hidden from him a few times and he has had to use his nose to find his owner, he will not only keep a careful watch to see that master does not disappear again, but it may well have given him the idea of getting his nose down to follow a line.

Apart from these enjoyable country walks, during which the pup will be learning to use his nose and become interested in various game scents, he should also be taken into town a few times to become accustomed to traffic, crowds of people etc. Of course, he is not likely to meet these hazards out shooting, but the more inured he can become to anything the modern world is likely to hurl at him, the less worried he will be by the unexpected and the greater attention he will be able to give to the job in hand.

These days, dogs are hardly ever welcome in shops, so it is unfortunately not possible to combine the weekly shopping with socialising the pup. Time must be made for a separate expedition. The younger the puppy, providing he has had his inoculations, the better, especially as it is highly desirable that people should stop and pet him, and they are more likely to do that with a young puppy. When he is at the stage that he will trot happily along the pavement, oblivious of the traffic thundering by, and will be pleased to stop and talk to anyone who wishes to fondle him, this part of his education can be considered complete. In later life, it may be necessary to take the dog into a town, possibly to visit a vet, and if a little trouble has been taken at the puppy stage, a greater problem in adult life can be avoided.

The owner must be the most important person or object in his pup's life. For this reason it is not a good idea to let children spend *too* much time playing with him. In term-time this is not likely to arise, as in the evening one hopes the pup will be with his owner, but during the holidays it would be a pity if the puppy spent all day rushing about with the children so that when his master came home all he wanted to do was to sleep. It should be explained to the family that the puppy is not merely a pet, and certainly not a toy, but is a highly complex creature which is being educated. They should therefore avoid doing anything which would interfere with what is being taught. It is especially important that they should not throw balls or any other object for the puppy, or chase him when he has anything in his mouth. Otherwise, children and puppies playing together can do each other a lot of good, provided, of course, that the children are gentle and considerate.

Untold difficulties can be created in future training by the wrong handling of the puppy in infancy. Some examples of this have already been given, such as how the puppy can inadvertently be punished for coming when called or for retrieving to hand, but incidents will constantly happen when the wrong reaction on someone's part can lay up trouble for the future. Everything that is done to and with the puppy should be aimed at guiding him along the lines he should go, just as everything that happens to the puppy influences him for good or ill. Even if one could keep him in a glass case until he was old enough to start serious training, it would not be desirable, because his brain would be stagnating. The aim in these early months should be to broaden his outlook and prepare him for life ahead, while discouraging undesirable behaviour and encouraging any tendency which will be useful later. Professional trainers prefer to start as far as possible with virgin material—that is, a young dog which has not been started along the wrong track by an unthinking owner. If training one's own dog, one can make the job infinitely easier by intelligent anticipation of the problems one may later have to face.

Many retriever puppies like to walk beside their owner holding his or her hand. Personally, I never discourage this, although it can be rather painful! For one thing, it is rather a charming gesture of affection on the part of the dog, and for another it is a golden opportunity of persuading him to hold something gently. Praise him as long as he is gentle, but as soon as he grips too tightly show disapproval. The favourable bond between the dog and one's hands should never be broken. Try to remember never to hit the dog, particularly in the face, with a bare hand, or to do anything which will destroy his trust in it. In later training it is vital for the dog to watch one's hands, while maintaining and strengthening eye contact, as mentioned earlier.

5 Elementary Training (Infant School)

The amateur training his own dog, as opposed to the professional training someone else's, need not suddenly wake up one morning and announce, 'Today I will start training my dog'. As previously explained, the training process is continuing all the time except when the dog is asleep. However, with a pup being trained along the lines suggested, the day *does* come when one must decide not to allow him to run in for the dummy any more. This can perhaps be regarded as the time when formal training starts.

Several factors should be taken into account in deciding when this moment has arrived. The main one is the temperament of the individual dog. If he is a tough, jolly extrovert, full of bounce and really keen on his dummies, an early start, at around six months, is indicated. On the whole, the more sensitive the pup, and the less keen on retrieving (not that these two points necessarily go together), the longer the 'all play and no compulsion' stage should last. It might be as well to explain what is meant by compulsion. It does not necessarily imply any degree of severity, but merely the imposing of the trainer's will over that of the puppy. A simple example is that of pushing him into the sitting position.

Provided that the puppy is having the sort of upbringing recommended, with plenty of mental stimulation and the right kind of discipline, the start of formal training can be left to a year old or later. Plenty of examples are known of dogs being successfully trained a good deal older than this. My own bitch

Manymills Lucky Charm, W.D.Ex., U.D.Ex., C.D.Ex., never had any formal gundog training until she was nearly five years old, although she had been trained for obedience and working trials, and been out rough shooting occasionally. She went on to win three open working tests and three field trials.

It is easier to start training a puppy in spring or early summer, as most people have more spare time during daylight hours then, and the likelihood of pleasant weather is more conducive to happy training for both parties.

It is not essential to give a lesson every day, and it is important never to continue for very long, especially when the pup is young. A few minutes twice a day are better than quarter of an hour daily, and a few days' break in training every so often is quite a good idea. Dogs do not quickly forget what they have learnt and one can carry on where one left off with a more receptive puppy.

One should never continue to the point of boredom, and because something is going well is no reason to repeat it more than two or three times. It is better to stop immediately the pup does something right, otherwise one runs the risk of getting a perfect response the first time, a less good one the second time, and a still worse one on the third occasion. This is just the opposite of what should be happening, and leads to a very difficult situation in which a decision has to be made either to stop when the puppy is not doing what it is known he can do, or to risk a further deterioration in performance by persisting.

The early lessons should preferably take place somewhere familiar to the puppy, but where there are no distractions and no audience. Later on, the pup must be capable of working and obeying where distractions abound, but to start with everything should be made as easy as possible, as it is highly desirable to build up a pattern of success.

Later on it may be very useful to join a gundog training class, if there is one in the area, but I see no point in turning up at class with a puppy which has had no training whatsoever. Classes are intended partly to train the novice trainer, and partly for everyone, novice and experienced handler alike, to accustom his dog to working in company. They also give the opportunity of varied retrieves on different grounds to which the amateur trainer would not otherwise have access, and teach the dog that a lot of his working life will be spent sitting still, while other dogs provide a sample of the distraction and temptation that he will later meet in the shooting field.

Depending on the capabilities of the trainer in charge, it might be possible to learn some very useful hints at classes, but too much should not be expected of them, owing to lack of time to deal with individual problems. However, the intelligent student can learn a very great deal by noting the successes and failures of his fellow handlers, and working out the reasons for them.

Even an experienced trainer like Mrs Purbrick still occasionally attends classes hoping to learn something, but she says some classes are cases of the blind attempting to lead the blind. Many trainers fail to instil into novices the importance of allowing for wind direction in handling dogs, for instance.

If gundog training classes are available, there is not much point in attending general obedience classes, as they can teach the potential gundog nothing of particular use to him except discipline and behaviour in the company of other dogs.

As well as being taught to mix without aggression or fear with other dogs, the young gundog should also be taught steadiness to farm stock and horses. He should be taken among them on a lead and scolded if he attempts to chase. If he shows fear, in the case of cows or horses, he should be quietly reassured and the treatment continued until he is reasonably relaxed and happy.

Several of the top trainers have all manner of livestock, from donkeys and ponies down to geese and guinea fowl, loose on their training grounds for the education of young dogs.

61

The trainer should equip himself with a number of dummies, at least some of which must float. They should vary in weight, size and material, preparing the young dog for the variety of game he will later have to pick up. Dummies can be made from logs of wood, covered with several layers of soft material, such as old socks. It is as well also to have one or two dummies of which the top layer is a rabbit or hare skin, but these should not be used to the exclusion of materials which are less interesting to the dog. Pheasant and duck wings can also be bound on to dummies, giving the first introduction to feather. Water dummies, which float high and are thus easily seen, can be made from old bleach or washing-up-liquid bottles, covered and weighted sufficiently for convenient throwing. The larger the variety of dummies a dog is trained on, the more broadminded he will become about what he picks up, and the less trouble is likely to be experienced in getting him to pick less usual forms of game in the shooting field. It is a good idea, when possible, to borrow other people's dummies, so that the pup does not get the idea that he is to retrieve only something bearing his owner's scent.

On the rare occasion when difficulty may be experienced in getting the young retriever to pick up any object at all, the method Mrs Radclyffe used with a reluctant youngster may be useful. She carried around with her for months a rolled-up pair of gloves, offering them to the bitch from time to time. At last they were accepted. Eventually the day came when the bitch picked them from the ground, and after that she never looked back. It is usually a matter of finding an object really attractive to the dog, and working on from there.

A whistle is the next essential. Some people prefer the so-called silent whistle (they are not actually silent, but very high-pitched so that the sound they emit is very quiet to a human ear, but supposedly very easily heard by a dog) and some prefer a whistle which they *know* is emitting a good loud blast which the dog two fields away can hear! The choice is up to the trainer, but in any case it is a good idea to start teaching the dog to respond to a fairly quiet blast, so that later on, if really necessary, a much louder noise can be produced, which one hopes will stop the dog in his tracks through sheer surprise. It is the same principle as previously mentioned in connection with not shouting at a dog except in case of dire emergency.

A long, light lead with a noose attached, preferably of chain if the dog is at all boisterous, and possibly a check cord, will complete the basic equipment. The latter may never be needed, but, if it is, can be made from a length of strong, light cord.

The first thing to teach the young pup is to sit on command. This can be done very young, at eight or nine weeks, but as a puppy of this age has not the concentration to remain sitting for long there is not much point. The fact that a dog will sit is of little use. The useful thing is that it will remain seated whatever the temptation, until given permission to get up.

Many intelligent retriever puppies can be taught to respond to the word 'sit' (or whatever alternative command has been chosen) in one or two lessons. The puppy should be taken to a quiet place without distractions and, when the trainer has his attention, he should say 'Sit' firmly but not angrily, and at the same time raise the pup's head with one hand under the chin, and with the other hand press the hindquarters downwards. As soon as the pup is in the sitting position, praise should be given. Restrain him in position for a few seconds, praising gently but without getting him too excited, and then release him with whatever word of release has been chosen. This can be repeated several times, and most puppies will quickly start to respond when hands are laid on them, even if they are not actually responding to the command. That will follow soon enough. With a very lively youngster, perhaps one whose training should have been started rather earlier, it may be easier to have the dog on a lead, and a slight backwards and upwards jerk under the chin may be combined with the downward push on the quarters. With this, or any not unduly sensitive type, response can be speeded up, once the dog really understands the command, by a light slap instead of the push on the quarters, if he does not obey immediately.

Once the puppy has learnt to sit promptly on command, and remain for a few seconds without attempting to get up, the next stage is to teach him to remain sitting while one walks away. It is essential always to have one eye on the puppy and to be ready immediately to go back to him if he moves, and replace him on the *exact* spot he left. One so often sees people leave a dog sitting or lying down and, when they walk away, the dog attempts to follow. Instead of rushing back and replacing the dog on the exact spot, they shout 'Sit' from where they are and, if the dog sits, no matter how many feet forward he may have moved, they are satisfied. The dog has thus gained a point and the trainer has lost one.

There is in fact no need to employ the slightest severity in teaching a dog to remain where he is put. It is merely a matter of constantly replacing him, and making sure that one's own obstinacy holds out longer than the dog's. Certainly, matters can be speeded up with a confident dog by being slightly cross as one replaces him, but this technique should not be used with one that gets up and follows through fear of being left.

The first time one attempts to leave the pup, one should not move away more than foot or two, and should go back immediately to praise the pup for staying. It is far better to build on a basis of praise for having stayed than scolding for having moved. It is a matter of judgement to know just how far one can go in moving away from the pup. Some are much easier to teach to stay on the drop than others. At some stage one should walk round behind the puppy, and be ready immediately to bend down and push him back if he tries to get up, as most of them do the first time this is attempted. One should be very confident about one's puppy's steadiness before attempting to go out of sight, and the first time the handler should just disappear momentarily behind a tree and go straight back to the pup again to praise him for staying.

One should never, or almost never, leave the pup sitting and then call him up, in the early stages. The reason is that he must be praised for *staying* and if he is called up, there is no opportunity to do this. It may be found that the staying lesson has been learnt so thoroughly that, when eventually an attempt to call him is made, he refuses to move! A little gentle persuasion will soon cure this.

Once the pup is steady on the drop, steadiness to thrown dummies can be taught. This is probably the most important lesson the young gundog ever learns, and is the cornerstone of good behaviour for the rest of his life. Any working-bred gundog will hunt and retrieve after a fashion, as witness the hundreds of dogs which are taken into the shooting field with no training whatsoever. It is knowing when *not* to retrieve that is the deciding factor between the trained dog and the unmitigated nuisance.

With all but the most biddable type of puppy, it is probably best to start with the pup on the lead. Having made him sit, the handler should throw the dummy a few yards. If the pup attempts to dash after it, as he almost certainly will, he should be stopped, scolded mildly, and replaced. The handler should retrieve the dummy himself and try again—and again—until success is achieved. When the puppy no longer attempts to run in, the lead can be removed, but it is important to be ready to intercept him if he once more tries to run in, as he may well do. Each time he must be firmly replaced on the exact spot from which he moved and scolded if he persists in moving. It is a matter of fine judgement to decide at what point to let the puppy have a retrieve. The more determined he was to run in, the longer a retrieve should be delayed. A sensitive pup, however, should be allowed one fairly soon to ensure that he is not being put off the dummy. In all cases the lesson should begin and end with a non-retrieve. The handler must be prepared, in training, to throw far more dummies than the dog is intended to retrieve. The handler then leaves the dog seated while picking the dummy himself. Because of the process of association of ideas in the dog's mind, one must avoid building up too much of a connection between a falling dummy (or bird) and a retrieve. Some association, of course, is inevitable.

The process of steadying the pup can be taken a stage further by rolling balls past him, throwing a dummy from behind to land in front of him when he is not expecting it, throwing several dummies all around him, and anything else the wit of the handler can devise. A dog which is not 100 per cent steady on dummies will never be so on the real thing, dummies being *so* much less tempting than game.

Plate 11 The Hon Mrs A. Jessel teaching one of her Flatcoats to walk to heel

Coincidentally with the foregoing, the pup can be learning to walk at heel. With some biddable, anxious-to-please youngsters, this can effectively be taught without the use of a lead at all. The handler should start with the pup sitting squarely at his left side, facing forwards, but with his eyes on the handler, who should say 'Heel' in a bright, encouraging voice, and walk smartly forward, the faster the better. The pup should be praised so long as he is in the right position, ie with his head in the vicinity of his handler's left knee. If he lags, the handler should not wait for him, but go faster still, encouraging him with his right hand. The occasional titbit can be useful to persuade the dog to keep close. If the puppy dashes in front, the handler should do a smart about-turn, thus putting the puppy behind him, and call him up in the same way as if he were lagging. If the pup walks wide to the left, the handler should turn right. The whole point is to get the dog working to the handler, not for the handler to fit in with the dog.

Most owners with most dogs, however, will probably find it easier to teach walking at heel with the use of a lead. The principle should remain the same, though, of encouraging the dog in towards one's left side, and the lead itself should be used as little as possible. Some training manuals advocate a lot of lead-jerking, but, unless very carefully timed and combined with lots of praise and encouragement, this can lead to a sulky dog hanging back because he has come to loathe heelwork. This must be avoided at all costs as it is an attitude much harder to cure than that of the over-boisterous dog which persists in getting too far in front. Some jerking may be employed with this type, but it is just as effective and much safer, though it may take longer, to do an about-turn *every* time the dog gets in front. He eventually learns that unless he keeps in the right position he and his owner will never get anywhere, but merely walk up and down on a small area. Heelwork sessions should be kept short, sharp and interesting. It is important to walk quickly to maintain the interest of the dog. The pace can be slowed later to one more in keeping with practical requirements. Every now and then, if only to enable the handler to recover his breath, a halt should be made and the dog required to sit smartly in position at the handler's left.

This is as good an opportunity as any of teaching the dog the rudiments of sitting to the whistle, as after a while he will have learnt to sit every time the handler halts. One sharp blast of the whistle can then be introduced as the dog sits, and he will quickly come to associate sound and action.

Most people use one long blast on the whistle as a signal to sit, or at least to stop, and a series of short double notes as a recall signal. The latter can be taught to a young puppy as soon as he is responding to his name, and in the same way. The recall whistle should be a pleasant and welcoming sound to the pup, and when he obeys, he should always be praised. At first, a titbit can be given as a reward for quick response to the recall whistle, and also as a refresher at any stage in training when the dog has slowed up in his reaction. Mrs Radclyffe likes to use titbits in this way to speed up recalls by rewarding the first dog to reach her, when several are running loose. Most trainers use food for this sort of thing, though never in connection with retrieving. Mrs Purbrick, however, is absolutely opposed to the use of edible rewards under any circumstances, being of the opinion that a pat or a caress should be enough.

Having taken care to buy a non-gunshy puppy, the introduction of bangs should not present any problems. However, it is most desirable that the puppy should have continued to hear gunfire, not in connection with anything in particular, from the time he left his breeder to the time serious training is started. If this has not happened, some caution should be used the first time a gun or starting pistol is fired. The best idea is to get someone else to fire it, at a considerable distance from the puppy, so that the owner is at hand to observe the reaction and to supply comforting words if necessary. If the pup exhibited no fear, a second shot can be fired slightly nearer. Next time try a first shot at the distance reached previously, and so on, until the pup can withstand the starting pistol or gun fired within a few yards. I prefer a starting pistol to a gun as the former can be practically hidden in the hand, and certainly fired from behind one's back, whereas a gun being brandished is in itself a somewhat threatening gesture to a sensitive puppy. When the noise is causing the pup no concern, the pistol can be fired and a thick stick held in the hands at the same time to simulate a gun, so that the pup can be gradually accustomed to the brandishing of a weapon.

If the dog shows real dislike of the sound of firing, great care must be taken that no kind of gun is ever fired during a training session. The bang must never come to be associated with retrieving, for fear of making the dog dislike the latter as much as the former. Instead, a shot from the starting pistol should become the prelude to feeding time, or being let out of the kennel, or anything else that the pup really enjoys other than his training. Shots can also be fired at random while the pup is running about enjoying himself and is at some distance from the handler. He can then be called up and rewarded with a titbit.

Methods such as these should be effective with all but the genuinely and incurably gunshy. It does not really matter if the dog's training gets to the stage of introduction to the shooting field before he has completely got over his fear of gunfire, so long as his reaction to a shot is merely to duck or lie down, and not to bolt. The excitement of a shooting day will help him to overcome any residual fear, although in a case like this the introduction to the real thing should be in the form of a day's picking up for the owner, so that the dog does not need to have a gun fired right over him. Pigeon hides and grouse butts should also be avoided at first for the same reason.

There is, of course, a lot to be said for having a dog whose reaction to a shot is to drop, or at least to hesitate, and Mr Wylie is emphatic that the gun-nervous dog, once cured of his fear, nearly always turns out to be a good one, as he is a dog with a conscience. He advises a gradual introduction to the shooting field from well behind the line, where wounded birds often come down. Picking runners earlier and more frequently than might be advisable with a bolder dog is very helpful in ridding a young dog of a dislike of gunfire. Even letting him run in may be tried, as a dog of this temperament will be easy enough to steady again later.

Some dogs dislike intensely the sound made by the mechanical dummy-thrower, which makes a bang and fires a dummy a considerable distance at the same time. These devices are extremely useful in teaching dogs to mark and in getting dummies to places which would otherwise be difficult, such as across water. If a dog really dislikes them, however, one should leave him sitting and go some distance away before firing, or not use them at all.

An easy, enjoyable lesson, which the dog can start as soon as he is physically ready, is jumping. A lightly built pup can start on low jumps as soon as he is old enough to begin any other training mentioned in this chapter, but a very heavily built one should not be asked to jump anything but the lowest heights until he is at least a year old. Most dogs love jumping. It makes the minimum demand on their brain power, so can be used as a relaxation for dog and handler, and it is an excellent method of getting on good terms with an older dog which one is starting to train. It is probably not worth constructing anything elaborate in the way of jumps if there is only one pupil, but, when no suitable low fence can be found, it is not difficult to devise something as low as 2ft in height to start with. If there is any way round the jump, the dog should be put on the lead. The handler can either step over the jump himself, or walk closely past the end of it, preventing the dog from doing the same. A command such as 'Over' must be decided upon and, as a height very easy for the dog will have been chosen, no great difficulty should be experienced in persuading him over it. If there is difficulty, use a lower jump. It does not matter if one has to go down to 1ft or less to get the pup started. Once he has the idea, he will delight in it, as it is such an easy way of pleasing his handler. Once he really knows what the word of command means, and is jumping on a loose lead, the lead can be abandoned. It can always be reverted to in the future with a different type of jump if the dog is reluctant.

It is a fallacy to think that teaching the dog to jump is going to make him jump out of his kennel or the garden, unless, of course, these fences are ridiculously low or are the ones the handler has been using for practice! Sooner or later it will be necessary for the dog to jump when out shooting, and nothing is more attractive than the willing and stylish jumper which does not waste time looking for a way round.

It has been suggested that several different lessons should be continuing in conjunction with each other. This all helps to prevent boredom, which is to be avoided at all costs. If the dog is becoming depressed with a surfeit of steadiness and sitting and staying, try some jumping or heelwork for a change. As well as ringing the changes in this way, training should take place in different locations. Nothing is more boring for a dog than always to be taken to exactly the same place to go through the same old routine. If the dog appears to be losing interest, there is no harm at all in stopping training for several weeks. The pupil will have forgotten nothing previously learnt, and will come back with renewed enthusiasm, as may the trainer too.

It is even possible that a cessation of training will consolidate in the dog's head what was previously not clear to him. This sounds rather far fetched, but does appear to happen. An illustration of this that I remember from my childhood occurred when I was trying to teach my pet Cocker to 'shake hands'. Very little progress appeared to have been made by the end of the holidays. However, when I returned home at the end of the following term, she raised her right paw immediately she was asked, and did so on every subsequent occasion without the slightest hesitation.

The aim should be to stretch the dog's brain, without over-straining it. A happy medium has to be found between trying to go too fast and overfacing the dog, and going too slowly and boring him by constant repetition of what he can already do. Each lesson should progress gradually and naturally to the next one. The young dog is always learning, so long as he is out of the kennel and with his owner.

If a misunderstanding occurs in training and the dog has an unpleasant experience, he will associate with the unpleasantness both the exercise he was carrying out at the time and the place in which it occurred. It thus behoves the trainer to take the greatest care that such mishaps do not occur, otherwise that particular training place will be useless for a long time, as the pup will not be happy there. He will also be reluctant to perform the exercise that he was carrying out at the time.

This quick association of ideas in the dog is the only basis upon which training can be accomplished, so it follows that the easier the dog is to train (because he associates exceptionally readily) the easier he will be to ruin, by letting him build up undesirable associations. Similarly, the more sensitive a dog, the more danger there is that a momentary loss of temper will have serious results that will take weeks or months to overcome.

Because the dog must associate command with appropriate action, it is vital to avoid in early training the giving of a command that one is not in a position to enforce. A simple example is blowing the 'stop' whistle when the dog is on the far side of a river. If the dog does not stop, there is nothing that the handler can do about it. The trainer should not allow himself to be put in this sort of a position until the dog is as nearly as possible completely reliable on the 'stop' whistle.

This never giving of a command without seeing that it is carried out is Mrs Atkinson's golden rule which she never breaks, although she succeeds when breaking some of the rules other trainers consider important.

It is also vital to allow the puppy to succeed *every* time in what he is asked to do, to maintain keenness. This involves not asking him to do anything beyond his capabilities and, if necessary, helping him to find the dummy which he has failed to locate on his own. Later on, of course, some failures are inevitable, especially in the shooting field, but to the youngster nothing succeeds like success. At the same time, it is annoying to have the sort of dog which 'won't come back without something in his mouth'. Nothing looks nicer, or speaks better for the trainer, than the dog which, when recalled after an unsuccessful hunt, gallops unhesitatingly and confidently up to his handler. There is no reason why this should not happen if it is remembered always, in all circumstances, to praise the dog for coming when he is called.

6 Something a Little More Difficult (Primary School)

The sooner the pup discovers that a retrieve can exist without him having seen anything thrown, the better. However, it is extraordinarily difficult to get some puppies to go forward and hunt for something unseen. A clear command and signal should already have been established for sending the pup off on a marked retrieve, and some puppies will go forward in a similar manner to hunt for a previously placed dummy the first time they are asked. It is most important that all the early unseen retrieves should be into the wind—ie, with the wind blowing from the dummy towards the handler and puppy. The dummy should not be immediately visible to the puppy, so a place should be chosen where the grass is not too short. It does not matter how close the first few unseen retrieves are; the object is merely to get the puppy going forward with the idea of a retrieve in his mind, and then succeeding in finding one. Of course, if he sets off in the wrong direction there is very little that can be done to correct him, as he has not yet learnt to stop on the whistle at any distance, or to take directions. To obviate this, the handler should at first tend to step forward with the puppy in the direction he wishes him to take. It is a good idea to make a clear signal with the arm held forward horizontally *before* sending the puppy. Some pups learn easily thus to go straight forward in the direction one is pointing. Others do not, but the signal is still worth making in the hope that eventually the message will get through.

If the puppy refuses to move forward at all for an unseen

74

retrieve, the handler will have to walk with him all the way to point out the dummy. If after a few attempts no progress is being made, there are various other methods that can be tried.

One method is to walk forward with the puppy at heel, on a lead if necessary, and let him see the dummy being dropped. He should be restrained from going for it, and walked on for a few yards until he appears to have forgotten about it. The handler should then about turn, and give the puppy the command and signal to retrieve. With any luck, he will suddenly remember the dummy. If not, it will be necessary to walk towards it with him as before. In a short while most puppies learn to remember the dummy for longer and longer distances, and can eventually be sent back for one they have not seen dropped.

When this method is being used, and on any other occasion when it is necessary to send a dog for a retrieve after he has been on the lead, great care should be taken that the removal of the lead is *never* allowed to become the signal to go. The lead should be removed and the puppy kept sitting for an appreciable time before being sent out. Otherwise, the removal of the lead comes to signify to the dog that he is free and can do what he likes. If this is allowed to happen, there is no chance at all of him ever being completely steady.

Another method of teaching unseens is to seat the puppy and throw out two or three dummies within a few yards of each other. He will easily retrieve one, but may need some persuasion to return to the area for a second and third. Eventually he will learn that when his handler sends him out in a certain direction for a retrieve, something will be found. It should be as long as possible before anything is allowed to happen to shatter this simple and touching faith.

Concurrently with the teaching of unseens and the increasing steadiness of the puppy, longer marked retrieves can be embarked upon. Most people (certainly most women) are incapable of throwing a dummy a suitable distance for any but the most elementary retrieving, while standing beside the dog. It is necessary to leave him on the drop and walk forward to throw the dummy, and then return to the dog before sending him out. One should avoid sending him to retrieve immediately on returning to his side. It is better to walk all round him and wait several seconds, and frequently to leave him seated while retrieving the dummy oneself, in order to maintain steadiness. The more the dog looks like running in, the less often he should be sent for a retrieve, and the longer he should be made to wait.

Some puppies go through a period of marking short. They will dash out to a certain distance and start hunting, refusing to go the extra few yards. This irritating phase nearly always disappears naturally, but its departure can be speeded up by always throwing the dummies into the wind, so that the dog is helped those last few yards by getting a whiff of scent. Try also to throw the dummy only just beyond the dog's natural limit, so that he succeeds in finding it, but only by going just that little bit further.

Otherwise, the length of marked retrieves should be varied constantly. The aim is to achieve an open-minded dog, which will use the evidence of his eyes and nose, not rely upon his knowledge of the distance that his handler normally throws the dummy.

It is important to start developing the dog's memory as soon as possible. There is nothing more useful than a dog which can remember by the end of a drive how many birds his master has shot, and where they are. Of course, few dogs ever get to the stage of being able to remember more than about four. The 'going back' exercise, described earlier in this chapter, is one memory-training device, and a fairly easy one as most dogs soon become very good at going back a long way for a dropped dummy which they have been allowed to mark. This is also a good exercise for speeding up delivery, especially if the handler continues to walk forward after despatching the dog. When the dog is sent for an unmarked dropped dummy, it is not so much a memory test as an exercise in following a line (the handler's), for the only way the dog will arrive at the dummy is by back-tracking on his owner's scent.

The practice of throwing out several dummies in the same area will also help to teach the pup to 'count' and remember that more than one dummy was thrown. Until the stage of teaching directional control is reached, it is not very easy to get the pup to retrieve two or more dummies thrown in different directions, but it can be tried. Most pups will retrieve correctly two dummies thrown in entirely opposite directions, but at lesser angles the tendency is to go for the last one they saw.

Mr Clitheroe always has his young dogs retrieving three marked dummies before he attempts to teach them to take directions. He does not mind in which order they are retrieved, the point is that the pupil should remember them.

Mr Male, on the other hand, hardly uses marked dummies at all. He likes to get his youngsters hunting for unseens as soon as possible.

A further method of developing memory is to throw out one or more dummies and then do a little heelwork. At first the puppy should be returned to the spot from which he originally marked before being sent out. Later on he can be sent from different positions.

It is to be hoped that by this time the puppy is delivering his dummies correctly at least 95 per cent of the time. If desired, he can be taught to sit in front to deliver. It does not really matter if he sits or stands, so long as he approaches the front of his handler without hesitation and holds his retrieves high for the handler to take. If the pup has been brought up and trained as suggested, no difficulty in achieving this should be experienced. However, there are some dogs (usually the diffident type) which naturally hang their heads on approach. In these cases it is probably better to teach the dog to sit, which tends to raise the head automatically, but the handler can assist by encouraging the dog and stroking him under the chin for several seconds before taking the dummy. If there is no tendency to drop the retrieve, a titbit can be offered

Plate 12 A good delivery by one of Mrs Radclyffe's Labradors

occasionally when the dog delivers correctly, but it can be imagined that most greedy pups will quickly start to spit the dummy out as soon as they reach the handler, in order to get the titbit. The use of titbits should therefore be discontinued as quickly as possible and certainly before this point is reached. Most trainers, in fact, would ban them altogether in a retrieving context.

A puppy which persistently drops the dummy at the handler's feet should be made to pick it up again, while the handler steps backwards and again attempts to obtain a correct delivery. If this does not work, the handler should walk or run away when the pup approaches, and continue to walk away while the dog carries the dummy alongside. If, when the handler stops, the pup then drops the dummy, the process should be repeated until it is possible to take the retrieve before it is dropped, whereupon the pup should be heartily praised.

In a very few cases neither of these methods is successful

and it will be necessary to teach the dog to 'hold' as a separate exercise, by putting the dummy in his mouth and holding it there. Should the dog succeed in spitting it out, it must be replaced, until resistance ceases. During this time *no* other retrieving should be taking place. However, the use of even the minimal force necessary to make the unwilling dog 'hold' is a highly skilled operation depending upon exact timing and a basically excellent relationship with the dog, so it should be avoided by beginners if at all possible. If necessary, an experienced trainer should be asked to demonstrate the procedure.

The opposite problem is the dog which holds on to dummies too tightly and is reluctant to give them up. This does not necessarily mean that the dog is going to be hard mouthed, but sooner or later the situation has got to be tackled. It is important first to make sure that the pup has got into the habit of coming straight in with the dummy before any steps are taken to cure his habit of gripping too tightly. Until this point has been reached, the handler should praise the dog for bringing the dummy and make no attempt to take it for some little time, as with any other type of puppy. The dummy should never be pulled from the dog's mouth, but, if he won't let go, the jaws should be opened by pressing the flews against the dog's back teeth. If, after a time, this does not bring about an improvement, a cure can be effected by stepping on one of the dog's front feet simultaneously with the command 'Dead' or 'Give' when the handler wishes him to release the dummy. This always seems to work, but naturally it will to some extent inhibit a happy approach and delivery, so should not be done more often nor more severely than absolutely necessary. It is, however, essential to achieve a willing release of the dummy before the dog is ever asked to retrieve game in any form.

A further refinement to the 100 per cent perfect retrieve and delivery, which must be achieved before thinking of trying the dog out on game, is to throw another dummy while the dog is returning with one in his mouth. If he attempts to dash after it, and particularly if he drops the one he is carrying, the required standard of discipline has not yet been reached. To begin with, the handler should throw the second dummy to one side and slightly behind himself, so that it is easy to intercept the puppy if he tries to go for it. Later on, the second dummy can be thrown nearer to the dog, or right across his path. There is still no guarantee, however reliable he becomes on this exercise, that he will not drop the bird he is carrying in order to run in on another that is shot, particularly if the latter is a runner; but at least the idea will have been put into his mind that such behaviour is wrong, and the handler will have some chance of stopping him.

Additional exercises in steadiness are walking with the dog at heel off the lead, and throwing the dummy suddenly in front of him. His automatic reaction should, after a few tries,

Plate 13   Mr Male likes to speed up his Labradors by sending two or three for a tennis ball together

be to stop and sit, and this should be insisted upon. A still more tempting variation is to throw out a dummy, or roll a ball, while the dog is running free. Again, the dog should be made to sit immediately he sees the dummy or ball.

Balls can be very useful; being smaller than dummies they can be carried about more easily and are slightly harder to find, thus teaching the dog to use his nose. A ball can be hit with a tennis racket a lot further than most people can throw one, and it is also harder to mark, being smaller. Mr R. G. Baldwin is famous for his use of a tennis racket and balls for dog training, and does his directional control entirely by this method. Mr Male uses a tennis ball too, especially on water. He also speeds his dogs up by sending two or three together for the same retrieve. Jealousy keeps them hunting longer and more enthusiastically than they might do on their own, but, unlike a dummy, it is almost impossible for one dog to snatch a ball from another's mouth.

There are specially made, large, heavy balls on the market which when rolled down a grassy slope produce a distinct line of scent for a dog to follow. The dog can be seated at the top of the slope and the ball thrown a few yards ahead, so that it bounces and then rolls out of his sight. When sent to retrieve, he will go to the last place he saw it disappear and, one hopes, then take the line. Of course, it is not as simple as that and young dogs vary immensely in the speed with which they catch on to the knack of following a line. Oddly enough, it is sometimes the least-promising pupil in other respects that turns out to have hidden talents at this game. There is no doubt at all that a genuine scent trail of crushed and disturbed herbage is produced. On one occasion my ball went a lot further than was intended down a slope of the South Downs, and an experienced bitch took the line for a good 300 yards just as if it had been a running pheasant.

Training should by now be taking place in a variety of places, with different natural features, such as hedges and ditches, of which use can be made to create slightly more complicated marked retrieves. At this stage it should not be expected that the dog will go through a thick hedge in order to find a dummy he has not marked.

If the owner has more than one dog, it should be possible to work them together in such a way that one dog will remain sitting while the other is sent for a retrieve. To begin with it may be necessary to put one on a lead as, until taught differently, the young dog will naturally assume that, when a command is given, he is to fetch the dummy. In this case the dog's name should always precede the order to retrieve and, if the puppy's steadiness lessons on his own have been thoroughly taught, it will not take long for him to realise that he is *only* to go when his name is called. An expert can work any number of dogs together in this way. Mrs Purbrick, in

Plate 14 Mrs Daphne Purbrick is famous for her demonstrations working five or six Labradors at once

particular, is very well known for her demonstrations in public with up to six dogs.

A very diffident puppy, the first time he is worked in company and prevented from going for what he genuinely thought was his retrieve, may be so upset that he will refuse to go forward when his turn comes. I had this problem once and cured it by the use of titbits. I sat several dogs in a row and threw a piece of biscuit for each in turn, which was good marking and nosework practice too. It soon resulted in the youngster overcoming her fear and going forward happily when her turn came.

Out shooting the temptation is very great for a dog to pretend he thought he heard his name, but one is aware that it is pretence because the same dog is rock steady on dummies! Names that sound similar should if possible be avoided, but it is surprising how dogs can distinguish between words that one might think would be confusing. I once had a 'Nelson' and an 'Elsa' at the same time, and each managed to distinguish its own name from the other.

There is nothing more maddening than for one dog to snatch a retrieve from another's mouth. This is one of the very quickest ways of producing hard mouth and of course a bird which has been the object of a tug-of-war is likely to be severely damaged. It also means that the meeker of the two dogs does not get credited with his retrieves. A watch should be kept right from the start to see that this does not happen with dummies. One dog should be placed so that the other has to pass within a few inches to deliver the dummy and, if the sitting dog attempts to interfere, he should be given a sharp slap and word of reproof. At other times one dog should be running loose while the other retrieves, and again a careful watch should be kept to see that there is no interference. Once the habit starts out in the shooting field it is virtually impossible to break, as both dogs are liable to be out of sight in cover and when one of them appears with a bird he is likely to be praised. He may have been getting away with the crime for some time before it is realised what is happening. The only answer then is to let only one dog hunt at a time. Even if they are sent off in different directions, the thief is likely to veer round to join the other dog as soon as he is out of the handler's sight.

Assuming that a start has been made on jumping, advantage can be taken of any suitable fence that is encountered when out for a walk or for training. The bigger the variety of obstacles the dog is asked to tackle in training, the less likely is he to refuse to jump anything new in later life. Solid obstacles, like walls that the dog can scramble on to and over, are much easier than such things as wire netting which have to be jumped cleanly, and the dog can tackle correspondingly higher obstacles of the former type. A young dog should not be over-strained or asked to jump anything he cannot manage fairly easily. Barbed wire should be avoided in training, but the more plain wire fences the dog has jumped, the more likely he is to clear barbed wire without getting tangled up in it, if ever it is essential for him to jump it. Most Forestry Commission plantations are surrounded by wire

Plate 15   Very young puppies can be taught to swim if weather conditions are favourable

netting fences of a very convenient height for training young dogs.

A start can be made on water training if the weather and time of year are suitable; it will make life much easier later on if the puppy is accustomed to swimming as young as possible. It is wiser to choose a warm day, or better still a really hot one, when the puppy is more likely to want to immerse himself. If he has never swum before, either take another dog to recover any dummies that might otherwise be lost, or tie a length of string on to the dummy so that it can be dragged back. It is very difficult not to let one's enthusiasm outrun one's discretion to the point of throwing the dummy just a yard or two further than the puppy is prepared to go!

If possible, a not too wide stream of varying depth should be chosen, and the first retrieve given across a shallow part in which the puppy will not need to swim. If he crosses without trouble, a deeper place can be tried in which he will have to take one or two strokes. If he refuses to enter the water, the handler can cross and walk away, calling to the puppy to follow. If he still refuses, it may be necessary to put the lead on and insist that he comes. When he discovers that his feet can still reach the bottom, he should get over his fear, and very gradually can be persuaded to cross in increasingly deeper places. Most retrievers love water and present no problems, but occasionally a nervous one is found which will require great patience and perseverance. Other water-loving dogs are a great help in these cases.

If no stream is available, a lake or pond with gradually shelving sides can be used instead, but these are not nearly so suitable for a water-shy dog, as the element of crossing to the haven of dry land on the opposite bank is absent. However, a dummy can be placed a foot or two into the water, then gradually further and further out as confidence increases. With the normal puppy, it is usually possible to finish the first lesson with a swim for a marked dummy of 5 or 6 yards, but it is easy to be over-confident and this is where the second dog or the string on the dummy will come in useful! As always, one should finish on a note of success, even if that means being content with a shorter retrieve than the maximum the puppy has already achieved. If the puppy is at all water-shy, it will help to let him run in to his first few retrieves. Steadiness can easily be re-established later.

7 How Far Have We Got? (Eleven-Plus)

The first watershed in training is the decision that no more running in is to be allowed. The second is to embark on directional control, which also involves the ability to stop the dog at a distance. It cannot be over-emphasised that no two puppies are alike, but in the majority of cases one would expect a Labrador pupil to be approaching a year old before this stage is reached, and other breeds probably older. Estimating whether the puppy is ready for more advanced training is partly a matter of instinct. However, the trainer may have noticed whether or not the puppy seems receptive to hand signals, as it is likely that he will sometimes have waved

Plate 16   Nursery training is the rock upon which to build

an arm in the direction of a hidden dummy, although he knew perfectly well that his pupil could not be expected to understand the signal.

Before progressing further it is important to make sure that the basics have been absorbed correctly and there is a solid foundation. To quote Mrs Purbrick, 'Nursery training is the rock upon which to build'.

The trainer should ask himself if the puppy is steady to dummies thrown close to him, over and past him, and to rolled balls. There is a distinct danger that, although he may be rock steady to temptations of this sort, he is still inclined to 'jump the gun' for a marked retrieve. The reason for this is probably that the handler, while having done his steadiness homework in the early stages, has, once his pupil is retrieving at a greater distance, made the mistake of sending him for every dummy thrown. Thus the puppy learns that a dummy thrown within, say, 10 yards is not to be retrieved, but one thrown at 30 or 40 yards almost certainly is. Thus he is far more inclined to run in on the latter.

Exactly the same situation can arise in the shooting field, when the dog will be perfectly steady to birds falling close, because he has learnt that his handler will collect those himself. He may not, however, be steady to birds at a greater distance, which he has learnt from experience he is always sent for. The moral is clear: do not send the dog for every retrieve, no matter what the distance.

It should be possible to seat the dog, throw one or more dummies, and then return and stand with him, at the same time carrying out various actions—such as putting one's hands in one's pockets and taking them out again, scratching one's head, blowing one's nose, shifting from one foot to the other, walking round the dog, sitting on the ground and getting up again and yawning and stretching—all without the dog showing any inclination to move. If he takes any of these movements as a signal to go, he is not really steady and further work should be put in until he is. It cannot be over-emphasised that temptation will be much greater in the field so no vestige of unsteadiness on dummies should be allowed to remain.

The dog should also be steady to the dummy thrown unexpectedly past him when running loose, as described in the last chapter.

It is assumed that he has been taught to sit when the whistle is blown, during heel-walking training. The difficult part is ensuring that he sits as soon as the whistle is blown, wherever he is. First attempts should take place when the dog is no more than a yard or two away, but not walking at heel or otherwise under orders. If he does not sit at the first pip, blow again and this time jump on him (not literally) and make him sit—unless the puppy is an ultra-sensitive type, in which case milder methods must be employed. Once he is sitting immediately within a few yards, the distance can gradually be increased, but at no time must the pupil be allowed to get away with a non-response. The handler must be agile enough to get to the puppy immediately, seize him and push him down on the exact spot he was when the whistle was first blown, blowing the whistle again as he does so. It is a counsel of perfection, but in theory a dog must never be allowed to get away with not stopping the first time the whistle is blown. Mr Bob Baldwin is particularly emphatic on this point. Once a dog finds that his handler is content with a response to the second blast, he will start ignoring that too. Eventually this leads to complete indifference to the frantic sounds emanating from his owner.

It is to be hoped that some elementary idea of direction has been inculcated by always, before sending him out, facing the dog in the direction of any hidden dummy one wishes him to find. It is not possible to make much progress with training the dog on blind retrieves until he can be stopped and re-directed.

The handler should be able to seat the dog and throw two dummies in completely opposite directions, and by standing beside the puppy and pointing at the dummy desired, the other thus being directly behind, ensure that he collects them in the order they were thrown. If the dog insists on whipping round and tearing off in the opposite direction (ie for the most recently thrown dummy), something is not quite right in the relationship between trainer and trained. By this stage the dog should be more aware of what is wanted and willing to oblige. If the puppy fails to carry out this exercise correctly, go back to the beginning and try to find out what went wrong, with the idea of putting it right before attempting to progress further. It might be as well to re-examine one's system of commands and signals, to make sure they are absolutely clear. A second opinion is often valuable on this. In fact it can be highly educational for one dog trainer to attempt to 'handle' another on to a blind retrieve, using the same commands and signals one would to a dog!

If, however, the dog sails through all the above tests with flying colours, one can contemplate embarking on the teaching of stopping and taking direction, with a fair degree of confidence.

8 Handling (Secondary School)

Many gundogs are never taught directional control at all and many owners who have spent a lot of money on buying a properly trained dog never make use of this part of its education. Either they think that directional control is a fancy circus trick only suitable for effete field trial dogs, or they feel too self-conscious to blow their whistles and wave their arms about in public. There is, of course, something to be said for the latter viewpoint, especially if the whistling and arm-waving is ignored by the dog! Otherwise, the handler of the fully trained dog can feel a quiet sense of triumph when his is the only one capable of being directed on to a bird the far side of a river or any other impassable obstacle.

A trained dog is intended to save his owner's legs, apart from retrieving runners and other birds that the owner would be unable to find by himself. On a grouse moor or in any open country it is most useful to be able to direct the dog a long distance to pick a bird which the handler has marked and he has not, especially if a steep climb down one hill and up another is involved. Also, a dog which will take directions on land will usually do so on water and this can be even more useful in order not to lose birds.

Before teaching a dog to take directions, it is essential that he is absolutely reliable on the stop whistle. Otherwise there is no way of preventing him from going for the wrong dummy, which would destroy the whole object of the exercise. Mr Wylie thinks that many people make the mistake of leaving whistle training until too late a stage of training.

If the pupil will stop at a distance of say 30 yards when there

91

are no distractions, the next step is to throw out a dummy, send the dog for it, and blow the whistle to stop him before he reaches it. The earlier the whistle is blown, the more likely the dog is to stop. If he does not do so, the handler should do his best to get out to the dog before he picks the dummy, in which case he can be dragged back to where he was when the whistle was originally blown, the whistle should be blown again, and the dog forcibly made to drop. If, however, he succeeded in getting to the dummy first, the handler should take it from him without comment, throw it back to where it was, and then take the dog to where he should have stopped, blow the whistle, give him a mild shaking if it seems appropriate, and make him drop.

Next time the whistle should be blown much earlier, when the dog has hardly left the handler's feet. If in this case he does not stop, it is much easier for the handler to get to him in time to do something about it, and it will be a very hard-headed dog which does not at least hesitate having been corrected once. With a very biddable and sensitive dog, care must be taken not to frighten him to the extent that he refuses to go out to retrieve at all, and stopping the dog on a dummy for which the handler has sent him should be practised only very occasionally, for fear of confusing him. There is also the danger of making a young dog slow and hesitant if this exercise is practised too much, but unless the handler can stop his dog on the way to a retrieve he is not under proper control.

A very keen, fast and hard-headed dog which does not respond to the methods described earlier will have to be put on a check-cord, although most trainers dislike check-cords and consider them a confession of defeat. The dog should be despatched for the retrieve in the normal way, and the whistle blown *just* before he reaches the end of the cord. As in all cases where a cord is used, care should be taken not to remove it until the lesson has well and truly sunk in, or the dog will develop two patterns of behaviour, one for when he is wearing the cord and one for when he is not. It may be possible to hoodwink the dog to some extent by putting a collar on him to make him think the cord is still there, or alternatively to put a cord and a collar and lead on him and remove the latter with a great flourish, so that he thinks he is free.

Plate 17   Mrs June Atkinson and F.T.Ch. Holway Barrister demonstrating obedience to the 'stop' whistle

A tip, which I believe originally came from the late Edgar Winter, was given to me in slightly different forms by Mrs Atkinson, Mrs Purbrick and Mr Eric Baldwin. The idea is to create a positive response to the whistle rather than a purely negative one, by stopping the dog when he is running loose and immediately throwing a ball or dummy. After a few moments on the drop, the dog is sent to retrieve. He is thus encouraged to stop and look at his handler with eager anticipation. Mrs Purbrick's variation of this is for one handler to be walking up with the dog at heel while somebody else throws a dummy behind. Alternatively, the handler can throw a dummy over his own shoulder.

When the handler is absolutely satisfied that the dog will stop, he can proceed to the next step. This is to seat the dog, and throw one dummy each side of him at a distance of 12 or 15 yards. This can be done on a lawn, as it does not matter if the dummies are in full view of the dog. In fact, it is essential that he should find them easily, as the exercise is purely in taking direction, it being desirable that the dog should be rewarded by finding the dummy instantly when he turns the right way.

Plate 18 Part of an exercise in taking direction: Mrs Atkinson holds out one arm horizontally in the direction of the dummy

With the dog seated, the handler should retreat about a dozen paces and hold out one arm horizontally in the direction of the first dummy thrown, giving whatever command he uses for the dog to fetch. One of four things will happen: the dog may go for the right dummy, go for the wrong dummy (which was the last thrown), return to the handler, or refuse to move at all! If he goes for the right dummy, he should be heartily praised, and then returned to where he was sitting and the dummy thrown out again. He should then be sent for the other, which he may by then have forgotten. If, however, he

94

succeeds in that too, the handler can congratulate himself on his extreme luck in having a puppy which is going to be easy to train from the point where the sheep tend to be sorted from the goats. Many puppies will prove very apt pupils at everything right up to this stage, and then a mental blockage seems to set in. Some get over it and some don't, but the natural direction takers are the ones that are a joy to train.

If, however, the pup immediately set off for the wrong dummy, the whistle should be blown and if the previous lesson was thoroughly learnt, he will stop. The handler should then go closer and repeat the command and signal. Every effort should be made to prevent the puppy picking the wrong dummy.

In many cases the puppy will get up and return almost to the handler's feet before setting off for either dummy. This does not matter at this stage, although it does not look nearly as impressive as when the dog goes straight to where it is directed. In order to get over this tendency, the handler should, at first, only step back a yard or two before giving the signal and gradually increase the distance as the puppy's confidence grows.

A few puppies will be so bewildered that they will not move at all, especially if they have never been sent for a retrieve from anywhere except the handler's side. The answer here is to move much nearer, and gently persuade the puppy to go.

When the puppy appears not to understand one's signals at all, or if he is of such a diffident disposition that it is necessary to go to great lengths to prevent him making a mistake in order to avoid the need for correction, the basics of directional control can be taught more slowly, but just as surely, with only one dummy at a time.

In this case I think it is just as well to start with a dummy thrown straight back, as with most dogs it is more difficult to get them to go further out in a straight line than it is to get them to go to right or left. The dog should be seated as before and one dummy thrown directly behind him. The handler should then retreat a little distance and send him for the retrieve, giving whatever command and signal has been decided upon, probably 'Get out' or 'Back', together with a pushing motion of the raised arm with the open palm towards the dog.

Plate 19 Mrs Atkinson and F.T.Ch. Holway Barrister demonstrating obedience to the command 'Get Out'

Similarly, left and right dummies can be placed, but only one or the other so that there is no possibility of the puppy making a mistake. When, after a while, he is taking off immediately and confidently for the dummy in all three directions, the same exercise can be tried with previously placed unseen dummies, taking care that the wind is blowing directly from the dummy towards the dog each time. When the message seems to have been absorbed thoroughly, the two marked dummies can be tried again, and finally a third so that the dog can be sent to either side or straight out as required. Try always to vary the order in which the dog is sent, otherwise an intelligent dog quickly gets to know which is to be the next one, so that he is relying on his memory rather than the handler's signals. The distance from the dog that the dummies are placed can be gradually increased, as should the handler's distance from the dog.

There are many variations which can be introduced into this exercise. As the dog becomes more proficient, he can be seated and a dummy thrown, and then sent for a previously placed unseen one in the opposite direction. It is essential that he should remain absolutely reliable at stopping on the whistle. The object is to get him thoroughly to understand the signals, so that in the shooting field it will be possible to send him for a runner which he has not marked, and to direct him the way it has gone, even if he has marked another bird in a different direction. The handler must be very careful always to use the same commands and signals for the same thing, and to make sure the latter are clearly visible to the dog. At first, therefore, the lessons should take place on open ground, though later on handling in various thicknesses of cover should be practised, in which case the dog will only be able to see part of the signals and will have to guess the rest. When dog and handler are really in tune, this is usually possible.

As an alternative to what is sometimes known as the 'three-card trick', the dog can be seated beside the handler and four dummies thrown out, as it were on the four points of the compass, dog and handler being in the centre. The handler should then face the dog squarely towards each dummy in turn, and point in its direction before sending the dog. Due allowance should be made for the wind, ie if the wind is blowing from left to right, the dog should be pointed slightly to the right of each dummy. This exercise is a great help both in developing memory and in teaching the dog to go out in a straight line in the direction he is pointed, a time-saver for long-distance retrieves in the open, and most useful for unseen retrieves from water and cover.

Care should be taken that all this 'square-bashing' is not allowed to depress and bore the dog too much. It is almost inevitable that it will slow him down to some extent, but this should not matter as there is no dog alive which does not open out to a considerable extent when he gets on to real game, so there must be something in hand to allow for this. The really spectacular performer on dummies is often uncontrollable in the field!

Mr Bob Baldwin does not mind how much his young dogs slow down on dummies, even to walking pace. He states that they will speed up within a week on the real thing. It must be remembered, however, that his type of dog is hard and tough. Most other trainers dislike the idea of their dogs slowing down or losing enthusiasm at any stage.

It is very easy for the handler unwittingly to continue too long with the three- or four-dummy trick. Each time the dog retrieves a dummy, the handler will throw it back to act as a distraction before sending him for the next one, so a definite decision has to be made to call a halt at some point and pick up the remaining dummies oneself. Great concentration on the part of both dog and handler is required for this exercise. It is almost impossible to give too short a lesson, provided success has been achieved, and very easy to overdo it. Some dogs, especially if they were never particularly keen on dummies, begin to show boredom and reluctance at this stage, and the trainer is then presented with a real problem. He can either give the dog a long rest—up to a month or two—and then try again, or he can resort to any stratagem he can think of to make the lessons more attractive to the dog. Some people will recommend keeping him completely confined to his kennel except for his actual training period, but personally I cannot approve of this. Mr Wylie suggests the use of dead birds instead of dummies. I once taught a dog to take directions by cutting his dinnertime paunch into three or more pieces, and doing directional control with that. I am glad to say that this did not result in him eating his birds when he put this lesson into practice in the field.

When the dog fully understands the signals for left, right and go straight back, and not before, real progress can be made in training on unseen dummies. It is a matter of putting into practice what the dog has learnt and, if the handler has succeeded in getting the lessons thoroughly into his pupil's head without causing boredom or undue depression, very rapid progress can now be made. Life will become much more interesting for both dog and owner, as widely different training grounds can be used, giving a great variety of retrieves. A typical session with a dog at this stage might consist of a session of heelwork, culminating in arrival at the desired position. The dog will then be left sitting while two or three dummies are thrown out, perhaps one in the open and two into cover. The dog collects these in the order indicated. The handler then leaves him on the drop and goes out of sight in order to place one or two unseens. At this stage, although the dummies might be in cover, they should be in such a position that the handler can see the dog until he is within scenting distance of them. By now the dog should not invariably be sent for retrieves into the wind, as he must learn to make allowances for wind himself. However, the handler should always be aware of the direction of the wind and act accordingly, ie he should direct the dog to a position downwind of the dummy rather than to the precise spot where it is lying. A dog has only to pass a foot or two the wrong side of an object to fail to locate it.

The aim should be to condition the dog always to obey any signal he is given. That is why it is very unwise to make signals to puppies which have not been taught what the signals mean, as they then learn to ignore them. Care should also be taken that the dog is still stopping instantly at the first blast of the whistle, although probably by now he will have ceased to sit. This is not particularly important, so long as he stops and looks. Some dogs will stop but continue to gaze blankly in the wrong direction, probably hoping to wind the dummy from where they are. The advice of Mr Male and Mr R. Baldwin about this sort of dog is to sell it! Certainly training is very much more difficult with a dog which will not look at its handler, but, depending on the temperament and the reason for non-attention, various stratagems can be tried. The first has already been mentioned, that is, to make the dog welcome the stop whistle by blowing it and then throwing out a retrieve. For a harder type dog which is just being naughty, the handler could try Mrs Radclyffe's advice—to run out and shake him. Certainly there is no point in giving commands or signals to a dog which is looking elsewhere. It is essential to get his full attention first.

If the dog stops but then attempts to move, the whistle should be blown again. Sometimes a dog will stop, and look, but start off again in the direction he had made up his mind to go, in opposition to what his handler is indicating to him. If, after a second halt and signal, he still continues to go the wrong way, the only answer is to stop him again and move sufficiently near to be in a position to insist that he goes in the direction desired. However, a dog should never be punished for disobeying a signal unless the handler is absolutely certain he understood it and was being deliberately disobedient, which with a properly trained puppy is not likely to happen very often. Most puppies, most of the time, aim to please, and what looks like flagrant disobedience is far more likely to be lack of comprehension, which punishment would only aggravate. It is impossible to lay down hard and fast rules about what to do in every situation in training. Much of the skill lies in being able to sum up the situation quickly and decide what is causing the problem. Only then is it possible to arrive at the correct solution.

9 When Everything Goes Wrong

At some stage in training the owner may realise that he has got the wrong dog, and the directional control stage is the one when this is most likely to become apparent. There are numerous reasons why a certain handler will fail with a certain dog, although there may be nothing intrinsically wrong with either dog or handler. Anyone who is impatient and liable to lose his temper is most unlikely to succeed with a very sensitive dog, as any loss of temper will result in a serious setback which will take a long time to get over. It usually ends up with a vicious circle in which the more nervous and unhappy the dog becomes, the more impatient grows the handler, so that the sooner they are separated the better.

The opposite situation is that of the gentle, non-dominant, probably female handler with the big, hard, boisterous dog, which requires a really firm hand and is never going to get it from his present owner. This type of dog usually ends up completely out of control. Should two such handlers meet and swap dogs, each would get a lot of pleasure out of a type really suited to him. The first would probably never need to lose his temper, as he would be able to give it an outlet every so often in shaking up the dog at the right time and in the right place, doing nothing but good thereby. The second handler could obtain much satisfaction from coaxing and building up the confidence of the other handler's discarded dog.

Apart from instances of handlers and dogs which are just not compatible, it is possible with the best will in the world to have bought a dog lacking the brain power to absorb any but the most elementary training. This is, of course, more likely to occur with a puppy bred from non-working stock, but can also happen in the best regulated families. Cheap, badly reared puppies can turn out to be very disappointing and any which have serious health problems should not be persevered with.

There is no disgrace in admitting defeat, and the handler should never be afraid to do so. He should try and assess honestly whether it is entirely the dog which is at fault or whether it is merely a matter of incompatability, and that some other handler might be able to succeed where he has failed.

Mr E. Baldwin states that there are a very few dogs which are slightly touched in the head and therefore untrainable. However, it is usually a case of fitting the right dog to the right handler. Somewhere there is the ideal dog for every trainer and, equally, somewhere there is the right trainer for almost every dog.

A pet home should be found for any dog which seems unlikely to make a successful gundog for anyone, provided that his temperament is basically good. Otherwise the hard decision to have him put down ought to be made, for his own sake as well as everybody else's. An unduly nervous or aggressive dog, which is likely to bite the postman or, worse still, a child, should be put out of harm's way rather than be allowed to be passed on from home to home, becoming more and more unhappy and bad-tempered and probably ending up permanently chained as a so-called 'guard dog'.

In the case of a dog which just happens to be wrong for his handler, no great difficulty should be experienced in finding him another home, particularly if he is well bred and has had some basic training. One handler's reject might be someone else's dog of a lifetime. It is probably worth offering the dog back to his breeder, who is likely to be able to place him with a suitable new owner. The dog himself will be much happier with someone who appreciates his mental type.

I find it very distressing to witness a partnership of dog and handler that is obviously wrong, where the owner either will not admit the fact or thinks there is some virtue in refusing to part with a dog once it is in his possession. Owners deceive themselves on this point. Even adult dogs can happily change homes, given a reasonable settling-in period, provided the new home suits them as well or better than the old one. A dog going from the wrong hands (for him) to the right ones becomes a changed character and an infinitely better adjusted one.

Plate 20   Mr F. Clitheroe and F.T.Ch. Hedenhampark Holcot Fay demonstrating the happy relationship essential between dog and handler

Mr Clitheroe stresses the point that it is essential for dog and handler really to *like* each other before they can get anywhere together.

103

It is very hard to make the decision to cut one's losses and part with a puppy one has not only grown fond of but has expended a lot of time and trouble upon, especially as one is unlikely to be able to find another dog old enough to train in time for the following season. Also, no doubt, there will be family pressures to contend with. However, it is better to be without a dog for one season than to be saddled for perhaps ten seasons with a dog that does not really suit one. It should be possible, with the experience gained, to make a better job of selecting the next puppy so that similar problems do not occur again.

Another possibility is that handler and dog have come to a full stop in training merely because of a single problem to which the answer cannot be found. Rather than having to undergo the trauma of discarding the dog completely, it will be well worth taking expert advice on the particular problem, even to the extent of sending the youngster to a professional trainer for a while, if it seems likely that he or she may succeed where the owner has failed.

10 Water Work

Water retrieving, like jumping, should be fun for both dog and owner, providing welcome light relief in training. Really hot summer days, when it would be foolish to ask the dog to exert himself to any great extent in other ways, are ideal for water work. There are usually enough fine, warm days even in an English summer for it never to be necessary to do water training in cold weather. This does not mean that later on the dog will refuse to enter water in the depths of winter in the course of his job, but it is always better to make the early stages of any aspect of training as easy and pleasant as possible.

If the pupil has not already had a gentle introduction to water, as described in Chapter 6, now is the time to make sure that he does. Real difficulty is seldom encountered unless the puppy has previously had a fright connected with water, such as falling into a pond where the sides were too steep for him to climb out. Owners who have ornamental ponds or swimming pools in their gardens, and who wish to prevent their puppies from entering them, have a slight problem in that they must impress upon their dogs that going into that particular water is wrong, but going into other water is right. I always hope to be able to introduce my own puppies to water *before* they take their first dip in the goldfish pond, but it hardly ever works that way. How many times a puppy has to be corrected before he learns that the pond is out of bounds is some measure of the intelligence, or perhaps more accurately the sensitivity, of an individual dog. With my puppies, the minimum so far has been twice, and the maximum half a dozen or so times.

My method is to take the puppy back to the pond on a lead, as soon as the crime has been discovered. This is not difficult when a dripping wet puppy suddenly appears at the back door. Although it is impossible to tell where the puppy got into the pond, one can see from the trail of drips where he left it, and this is the place to which I lead him, jerking the lead hard just as he arrives at the brink. He is then given a good shaking and scolding. On the second and any subsequent occasions the puppy is also led right round the pond, and several shakings and scoldings are administered en route. The object is to make him associate that particular area of the garden with something unpleasant, so that he will avoid it altogether.

As soon as possible the puppy is taken with other dogs to the nearest available water and encouraged to go in with them. Very often this stage is reached with puppies of three months old or less, and even at that age they can be given a mini-retrieve of a yard or two.

With an older puppy that has learnt steadiness, he may be seated on the bank of the stream or lake and the first dummy thrown no more than a yard into the water. If no swimming is needed to recover the dummy, so much the better. The length of retrieves can very gradually be increased, if no trouble is encountered; but, as mentioned before, it is as well to have a reliable water-retrieving dog available or to tie a string to the dummy so that it may be recovered should the pupil refuse to go for it.

An immense amount of patience is required with genuinely water-shy dogs, but there is hardly a retriever alive which cannot eventually be persuaded to swim well and far enough to satisfy most owners. Mr Wylie says that a really water-shy dog has to be taught that it can swim. One of the most difficult he ever had, which was really terrified, had to be forced into water on a lead. It eventually became one of his best water dogs.

Mr Eric Baldwin gives similar advice. As a last resort, he recommends gently lowering the dog into water from a boat.

However, he emphasizes that no roughness should ever be employed, a sentiment echoed by every other successful trainer. The dog is already frightened. To terrify him further by a display of bad temper or impatience would only make matters far worse. Anyone who throws, pushes or kicks his dog into water does not deserve to succeed, and most certainly will not do so.

Once the dog is happily swimming as far as the handler is capable of throwing the dummy, some variations can be introduced in just the same way as retrieves on land should be varied.

A dog which understands about going out for unseen dummies on land should be equally capable of doing so on water, so long as he is willing to take to the water when ordered without the encouragement of a thrown dummy. If at first he will not, make the unseen retrieve very short, so that, although he has not seen it thrown, if he looks he should be able to see it floating. Alternatively, two or three dummies can be thrown out, so that the first is a simple marked retrieve but the others are more in the nature of an unseen or a memory test.

A dog which will stop to the whistle and will handle on land should do the same in water. Naturally it will not be possible for the dog to sit, or even stop dead, but most dogs will turn to face the handler when the whistle is blown and will take direction quite satisfactorily, so long as they are confident in the water. Many dogs, in fact, handle better on water than they do on land. For one thing, there are fewer distractions in the form of scent and, for another, it is not possible for them to go nearly so fast. However, if the dog does not stop to the whistle on water the first time it is attempted, a check-cord should be used so that he does not make the discovery that disobedience on water goes unpunished because the handler cannot get to him.

Great care must be taken that the cord does not get tangled up with the dog's legs, or frighten him in any way. It is merely necessary to pull him gently round in the water when the whistle is blown, in order to show him that he is required to turn and look when he hears it.

On one of the shoots where I used to pick up, there is a large lake; at one drive two guns stand on a road by the lake with a wall between them and the water, so that their dogs are in no position to mark. It may interest anti-field triallers to know that these guns invariably called for the services of the two pickers-up who ran in trials, to help them gather their birds after this drive, knowing that theirs would be the dogs which would swim out any distance and in any direction indicated for birds they had been unable to mark. This performance always brought the house down, although there is nothing at all difficult about it and most dogs could be taught to do the same if their owners took the trouble.

Another situation which sorts the sheep from the goats, or the men from the boys, is that of a bird down a long way out on the far side of a river. Very few gundogs are capable of picking this sort of bird, because they have never been taught to take direction at any distance. Unfortunately it does not take most of them very long to discover that once they are on the far side of water their handlers cannot get at them, and therefore they tend to take a lot less notice of the whistle and of signals. Once the dog has crossed the river, it is as well to let him stop and shake before trying to get his attention. If he has thoroughly learnt his getting back and side-to-side signals, it should be possible to handle him to the bird if it has landed within sight.

A river with a footbridge not too far away, but not so close that the dog is tempted to use it, is useful for practising this sort of thing, as if the worst comes to the worst the handler *can* get across the river to his dog and administer a forcible reminder that he is supposed to do as he is told, even on the far side of water.

Some handlers experience difficulty in getting their dogs out of water at the far side of a river to retrieve a dummy on the bank and, equally, in getting them to enter the water again carrying the retrieve. This is almost certainly the result of using only lakes or ponds for initial training, so the dog gets into the habit of expecting the retrieve always to be floating on the water. The problem is never likely to arise if the dog is trained to retrieve across a narrow stream very early, before too much work is done on retrieving from larger areas of water.

Longer retrieves can be provided by the use of the mechanical dummy-thrower, or alternatively by leaving the dog seated at one side of a pond or lake while the handler walks round and throws the retrieve in from the far side. In this case most intelligent dogs—although they will enter the water and swim out for the dummy because that is what they have been told to do—will land at the nearest point at the far side and return by the same route that the handler took. This is *not* water shyness, but shows a laudable desire to return as speedily as possible with the retrieve. I would never penalise a dog which did this at any working test or field trial I was judging, nor would any of the trainers mentioned in this book, all of whom are senior field trial judges.

Double and treble dummies on water should be practised, preferably on areas with no current so that the dummies stay more or less where they are thrown.

If one's dog is to be used for wildfowling on the shore he should be introduced to sea conditions as well as fresh water. Some dogs, which show no fear on inland water, hate the waves; the only answer is to get them gradually accustomed to increasingly rough water as gently as possible, starting on a fine, warm, calm day. The same applies to rivers and streams with strong currents. Many dogs dislike and fear them until they have been accustomed, by plenty of practice, to such conditions.

It is most important to try and avoid a young dog being put off water by any unpleasant experience. Dogs wearing collars should never be worked in cover in case they get caught up,

109

and it is even more horrifying to see dogs sent into water wearing loose chain collars, in which they could easily catch their forefeet. Dogs which jump into water also run the risk of impaling themselves on hidden stakes under the surface, so a gentle entry is to be encouraged if possible.

It is also possible to damage a dog's confidence by giving him too long a swim, so that he becomes frightened and exhausted. A young bitch of mine was once doing well in an open working test, when in the run-off she was asked to collect two long unseens in water. She failed on both and, whether it was merely the failure and consequent confusion or whether she struck something under the water and had a fright, the result was that it was not possible afterwards to get her to go more than about 20 yards for an unseen in water.

It should be remembered that long swims are exceedingly fatiguing for dogs unaccustomed to them, especially if the swim culminates in a steep climb up a bank. It is therefore extremely unwise to give many such retrieves in a training session. Probably three should be the absolute maximum, and then only if the pupil is given a rest between each one.

Many dogs, when leaving the water with a dummy or bird, will stop and shake as soon as they reach dry land, and some will put the retrieve down in order to do so. For the ordinary shooting man this probably does not matter, but if the aim is to take part in tests or trials the dog must deliver perfectly. One is assuming that, if he came out of the water with a live bird, the dog would have more sense than to put it down. In order to avoid this risk, it is just as well to try and get him to retrieve right up to hand, wet or dry.

If it is seen that the dog has begun to hesitate, the handler should on no account step forward and try to snatch the dummy before it is dropped, but should instead turn and run away, calling him to follow. If it is possible to get him to deliver properly this should be done, otherwise the dummy should be taken while handler and dog are still on the move. It is a mistake to stand too near the water's edge to await the

Plate 21 Some dogs insist upon putting down their retrieves when reaching dry land, in order to shake

Plate 22 The author's young Labrador shows that a perfect delivery from water is not impossible

dog; it is better to give him a fairly long run-in and then he will be in a greater hurry to reach his handler. A dog which has been taught to deliver correctly in his early training does not usually need much persuasion to learn that a similar delivery is required even when he is wet.

Mrs Atkinson thinks that many trainers make matters worse by fussing too much. If they bellow 'Hold' to the dog as he emerges from the water (a command which he probably has no reason to comprehend) he is all the more likely to hesitate and drop the dummy, It is easier not to let this habit start than to cure it, a rule which applies to nearly all bad habits in training.

11 Advanced Retrieving (Sixth Form)

Now the foundation has been laid, the endless and fascinating task of building upon it can begin. Personally I enjoy this stage of training much more than the sometimes wearisome, repetitive early lessons. If the pupil has got as far as this without serious snags, there is an excellent chance of him making a first-class mature worker, provided he does not develop a fault such as hard mouth or whining.

The aim now should be to take the dog about as much as possible into different types of cover and use the landscape to provide a great variety of retrieves. The pupil should by this time be capable of marking and remembering dummies of varying distances, in cover and in the open, beyond hedges and ditches, and into woods. The mechanical dummy-launcher is very useful for teaching him to mark by sound, if it is fired into woodland. The dog will not be able to see the dummy fall but will hear it, and after a while will learn to judge how far out to hunt. To begin with, the dummy should not be propelled too far into the cover, as the pupil will for the first time have to hunt on his own initiative with no help from his handler. The latter will not know whether the dog is hunting in the right place or not, until he appears with the dummy. The dog should not be recalled or given extra commands unless he reappears without the dummy, in which case he should be sent back to look for it again.

It will be found that a dog which has been taught to go straight out in the direction indicated for an unseen in the open will quickly adapt this skill to work in cover. However, he is far more likely to be side-tracked into following game scents when out of sight of his handler. Sooner or later he has to learn to use his own initiative and find his retrieves without help, although it must be borne in mind that initiative increases by leaps and bounds as soon as the dog is working on the real thing, so the emphasis at this stage of training must still be on discipline, obedience and control rather than on initiative and self-reliance.

The pupil must also learn to accept directions in partial cover, ie in thin woodland, bracken, or under any other conditions where he will be able to see the handler only part of the time. It is extremely difficult to time the whistle signal so that the dog stops at a point where he can see and be seen. Nine times out of ten, even if the whistle is blown when the dog is in sight, by the time he stops he is behind a tree or bush. The handler can either wait until the dog moves and then attract his attention, or move himself until he and the pupil can see each other. The dog must learn that in these cases the handler is trying to help, not hinder, and thus be inclined to want to put himself in a position where he can see. It is very gratifying the first time the young dog in training stops of his own accord and looks for directions, maddening though it can be when he does it too much and will not get out and hunt. The handler must learn to judge how often to give a direction: more for the hard-headed type which is reluctant to stop, and less for the over-reliant type which tends to stop and look for help too much.

One of the hardest things a dog can be called upon to do is to go out through cover and hunt in the open beyond it. His inclination is naturally to stay in the thick, rather than go through it and out the other side, especially under conditions where the handler cannot see what the dog is doing. The answer to this one is to make sure the pupil will always obey the command 'Get out', whether he is in sight or not. Futhermore, plenty of marked dummies beyond thick hedges, belts of trees etc, should be given before unseens of this type are attempted. This is another aspect of training for which the mechanical dummy-thrower is extremely valuable. Failing this, an assistant capable of throwing dummies really high is almost essential.

It is impossible for the lone trainer to teach his dog what will be required of him when walking up. For this operation, at least two helpers are needed: one to walk ahead and throw the dummies, and another with a dog also walking in line at heel. This is where gundog training classes can be extremely useful. There are normally at least ten or a dozen handlers and dogs per class, plus someone to throw dummies and someone else to fire at them. If there are no training classes within reach, it may be possible to find other people in the locality with young dogs at the same stage. The breeder of a puppy can often help by putting buyers of members of the same litter in touch with each other.

The dog must learn that he is to be steady to thrown dummies when he is walking at heel, just as he is when sitting still. He must also remain steady when other dogs are sent out to retrieve from a position close to him. Marking, too, is more difficult for the dog when walking than when sitting, until he has had practice at it. Now is the time when the handler will discover whether his heelwork training has been adequate; if it has not, there will still be time to polish it up before the dog sets foot in the shooting field, where it is important that he will keep to heel without constant nagging.

The pupil should by now be jumping freely and unhesitatingly over any obstacle of reasonable dimensions, and no opportunity should be missed of enlarging his education in this direction. I do not like my dogs jumping gates, or any sort of barred fence where it is possible for them to slip and get their hind legs caught, unless I am standing by to help if necessary. With this exception, however, and that of barbed wire, dogs should be taught to jump at a distance from their handlers. It is quite possible that it might be necessary to send the dog over two fences, or over a river and a fence, so that the handler cannot be close to the dog when he reaches the second

115

Plate 23 A trained dog (F.T.Ch. Holway Barrister) showing his ability to clear any obstacle likely to be encountered in the shooting field

obstacle. It is very much harder to get a dog to jump at a distance, especially for an unmarked bird, so this should be practised. It is not at all uncommon at a field trial to see a dog failing on a comparatively simple bird which has fallen the far side of a fence, and being easily eyewiped by the next dog whose jumping education has not been neglected.

The dog should be prepared, if ordered, to return to the same area again and again to look for dummies. On a big covert shoot it is quite usual for many birds to fall in the same area, and the young dog should be educated to accept that the fact that he has made one retrieve from a certain place does not mean there are no further retrieves there. One can lay on a lesson of this sort quite easily by placing a number of unseen dummies in an area of woodland and bringing the dog out later to look for them. It is unlikely that the handler will remember exactly where each one is, which is all to the good, as he will then be forced to let the dog hunt the area on his own initiative until all the dummies have been recovered.

Often on a shooting day birds are hung up in cover and never reach the ground. The height at which a dog can scent them depends on wind conditions, but all young dogs should be taught that it is possible for the retrieve to be somewhere other than on the ground. To begin with, the dummy should be placed in a bush only a foot or so above the ground, and in such a position that the handler can see to direct the dog right to the spot. Later on, it can be placed higher. As an alternative, the trainer can let the dog see him place the dummy, and send him back for it as he has been accustomed in the past. Some dogs get very clever at shaking dummies (and birds) down from a considerable height.

Some dogs, after a season or two in the field, learn to bark at the lightly wounded runners which succeed in fluttering up into trees or bushes out of the dog's reach. My own W.T.Ch. Manymills Tanne is a specialist at this, but unfortunately she is not always right, and many is the wild goose chase I have had into the depths of a wood, only for the bird to fly away on my arrival. This tends to happen early in the season with young birds which do not bother to fly right away from the dog but merely flutter up out of reach. When one dog has learnt to indicate such birds by barking, the others often follow suit. I have one which is rock steady except when he hears Tanne giving tongue. He then takes off at speed to join in the cacophony, and this can be extremely embarrassing. Occasionally he trees a bird himself and barks. On one occasion, I heard him barking rather uncertainly and when I went to investigate found him gazing up at an old woodpigeon's nest! This proved that he had learnt to look upwards to see if there were any unusual shapes silhouetted against the sky, which is interesting as one might have expected a dog to use his nose rather than his eyes in this sort of situation.

117

Sooner or later the youngster must be taught not to chase rabbits, or at least the fact that chasing them is wrong, which is not necessarily the same thing. If a dog is ever likely to be asked to retrieve a wounded rabbit or hare, then there are times when he must be allowed to chase. Of course, ideally the game should be shot again and killed, but this is not always possible. It is surprising that dogs can be taught to distinguish as well as they do when chasing is allowed and when it is not; this distinction must also be made in the case of a wounded bird which can just fly and an unwounded but low-flying one.

Most owners will be satisfied if their dog refrains from getting up and chasing any rabbit or hare which flashes past during a drive, and if he can be stopped on the whistle when he comes across a rabbit or hare while hunting for a retrieve. Nearly all dogs, if they are hunting in cover and put up a rabbit, will chase it into the open, but if they have been taught that chasing is wrong they can be stopped as soon as the handler sees what is happening and either shouts or blows the whistle.

Rabbit pens are extremely useful for teaching this lesson. However, few amateurs will wish to go to the trouble or expense of constructing one. It is usually possible, by asking among dog-minded keepers and other trainers, to find someone who has a pen and will allow it to be used. One brief lesson in the pen is a great deal better than nothing, and few retrievers need more than two or three, preferably in different pens and at fairly long intervals, to get the message that rabbits are not to be chased—at least, not when master is looking! Refresher courses in the pen in later life can also be most useful.

The first time the dog is taken into the pen he should be on a lead, if only for the protection of the rabbits. Handler and dog should walk round the pen until a rabbit gets up and runs in front of them, whereupon the pupil should be made smartly to sit. If he lunges forward and attempts to chase, he should be jerked back and scolded. If the previous lessons on steadiness to rolling balls and dummies were thoroughly learnt, it should not be long before the lead can be dispensed with, although the handler should remain extremely alert and ready to jump on the dog if necessary.

Plate 24   Discipline in the rabbit pen: the young dog remains steady while a rabbit runs past

The next stage is to leave the dog sitting and chase a rabbit past him. If there is any doubt about his behaviour, an assistant should do the chasing and the handler be near enough to intercept the dog if he moves. The only dogs likely to cause a great deal of trouble are those which have been allowed to go off hunting by themselves and are thus already hardened rabbit chasers. It is very unlikely that these can ever be made rabbit-proof, even if perfect behaviour in the pen is achieved. It can thus be seen that it is important not to let a prospective gundog go off hunting by himself or, worse still, with other dogs. Some youngsters, even without previous rabbit-chasing experience, prove to be extremely rabbit-minded and will take longer to steady down than others.

Once the dog is steady both at heel and when seated, a dummy can be thrown near a rabbit and the dog sent for it. The handler must be ready, whistle to lips, to stop the dog should he decide to go for the rabbit rather than the dummy.

Plate 25   The dog should stop automatically when a rabbit gets up

In fact, with many dogs which have been stopped on rabbits sufficiently often, it will prove more difficult to get them to go near enough to the rabbit to pick up the dummy than to stop them chasing. Some dogs will realise that it is the dummy and not the rabbit which is wanted, and will pick the former perfectly, but will then be unable to resist pursuing the rabbit for a yard or two, dummy in mouth! The final stage in the pen, if it is large enough, is to let the dog run about free and put up a rabbit at a distance from the handler. He *should* stop automatically. However, dogs learn about pens very quickly and the chances are that after the discipline which has been imposed the dog will refuse to run about naturally. He will be constantly anticipating the stop whistle so, however immaculate is the dog's behaviour in the pen, it must still be expected that he will chase a wild rabbit the first time he meets one. Even so, he should obey the stop whistle and connect his rabbit-pen lessons with the scolding his handler can then administer.

Some people keep only tame rabbits in their pens; although they are a great deal better than nothing, these do not run at anything like the speed of wild rabbits and so do not offer the same temptation. Some pen rabbits get so blasé about dogs that they refuse to run at all! Every effort should be made, therefore, to take the dog to places where he will encounter wild rabbits and be taught not to chase in a natural environment. No rabbit pen, no matter how large, can genuinely reproduce the real thing.

Hares run in a completely different way from rabbits and therefore a dog which is steady to one will not necessarily be so to the other. No gundog can be considered fully educated until it has seen plenty of hares in their natural environment and been firmly taught not to chase them.

Plate 26 Mr Andrew Wylie, who keeps a variety of livestock in his rabbit pen

The trainers interviewed for this book vary greatly in their use of rabbit pens. Three never use them, two only occasionally, and four use them quite a lot. Mr E. Baldwin thinks that people tend to be too harsh with their dogs in rabbit pens. Mr Wylie says that if a young dog sees rabbits often enough he will learn to treat them in the same way as poultry. In fact, many kinds of livestock are kept in the Wylie pen, and I found that a bitch of mine with one season's experience was far more intrigued by his guinea-fowl than by the rabbits.

An incident which illustrates the value of rabbit-pen training for young dogs happened when six Labradors of various ages were running loose in a field at some distance from me. I saw a rabbit run across in front of them and disappear into a wood. It was impossible to tell how many of the dogs saw it, but certainly one did—a two-year-old which on the previous day had had the second training session of his career in a rabbit pen, the first having taken place a year previously. Although I blew my whistle as soon as I noticed the rabbit, the dog had already stopped and was looking back at me. My pleasure was as great as my amazement. Certainly, had he not been in the pen the previous day, I am quite sure that he would have chased the rabbit, although he would probably have stopped when the whistle was blown.

It is a good idea to give a young dog some idea of how to follow a line before expecting him to follow and retrieve a runner in the shooting field. Most dogs that are exercised in the country will already have started to teach themselves this, by following up any fresh scents they happen to come across. However, as it is highly undesirable to allow them to give chase if and when they catch up with whatever they are trailing, these early attempts do not meet with any success and therefore go unrewarded, except for the pleasure the dog gets out of the actual following of the line. Various methods can be tried of giving a dog a line to follow which will end with a successful retrieve. The simplest has already been described:

that of sending the dog back on one's own track to retrieve a previously dropped dummy. However, a human being makes a much stronger scent trail than any bird or small animal, if only because a man's much greater weight results in a far heavier impression being made in the form of crushed herbage and disturbed ground, which is one of the elements of scent that a dog follows.

To make a lighter trail, more like the real thing, a dummy or dead bird or rabbit on the end of a line can be used, and this is Mr Male's method. The dummy or bird can be thrown out, preferably in a grass field, the handler keeping hold of the end of the line. The object can then be dragged towards the handler, taken off the line, and left. The dog is subsequently directed to the place where it fell, from the opposite side to where it is lying. With any luck he will find the fall and then work out the line. This is not an ideal method as the handler's scent blowing about will tend to obscure the trail of the dummy, unless the trial is laid in the same direction as the wind, which will make it much harder for the dog to track. An alternative method is for two people to drag along a dummy suspended on a long cord held between them. Here again, unless the cord is very long, human scent will tend to interfere with the track. A third method is the use of a heavy ball rolled down a slope, as described in Chapter 6.

Before he goes into the shooting field, the dog should have had some experience of retrieving cold game. Out of season, of course, there is a limit to what will be available for practice, though a friendly keeper may be able to provide a laying-pen casualty. Even corpses picked up on the road can be valuable, if they are not too damaged. A partridge, a grouse or a young hen pheasant are ideal to start with, as they are not too heavy and awkward. Failing any of these, Mrs Atkinson suggests using a jay, magpie or starling. As these are less attractive to a dog than game, if he will pick them he is unlikely to refuse to pick anything else, including woodcock.

Most dogs will retrieve a clean, cold bird the first time it is

123

thrown for them. I say 'thrown' deliberately, as a dog is more likely to retrieve something he sees thrown than something which is merely placed on the ground. If he will not pick it, a gradual transfer from dummy to bird can be made by enclosing the bird in a sock. When the dog is picking, carrying and delivering this quite happily, a thin nylon stocking can be substituted for the sock. Eventually the bird can be used with just one band of material holding its wings close against the body. It is, however, not a good thing to ask a dog to retrieve the same bird too many times, in case he becomes bored and sick of it. Equally, the same bird must not be used over such a long period that it begins to go high, or the dog will be more likely to eat it or roll on it than to retrieve it.

A clean, non-bloody rabbit can be used as a start, if there is no bird available, but the fact that a dog will retrieve fur is no guarantee that he will retrieve feather, and he must be taught to retrieve birds at some point. Retrieving fur rarely presents problems, except that dogs must learn correctly to balance hares. Wounded hares are a different problem, however, and many dogs do fight shy of them.

A woodpigeon can be used as a positively last resort for the first retrieve, but it is not a good species to start on as the feathers are so loose that they come off in the dog's mouth, encouraging him to spit the bird out or to mess about with his retrieves.

Duck and woodcock are less attractive to dogs than most other game birds, so youngsters should be taught to pick and carry them at the first available opportunity.

The next step is to retrieve a warm, freshly shot but definitely dead bird. As the majority of young dogs are likely to reach this stage of their training in the late summer, most people will be forced to use a pigeon in spite of the disadvantages already described. Therefore, if at all possible, cold birds of other species should have been practised upon first.

Finally, in the shooting field, a progression will have to be made from dead birds to live ones. This often happens naturally, but in home environments such as mine, where pet birds and poultry abound, the young dog has been brought up not to chase (and in my case has probably been severely disciplined by the parrot if he tried to become too familiar), so definite training in the retrieving of live birds is necessary.

Some young dogs will damage the first bird, live or dead, they get in their mouths, but if they are not tried with another for some time may be perfectly all right in the end. There is no real cure for hard mouth, and if the dog really damages birds he is useless as a retriever. Some impression can usually be formed during training as to whether a dog is likely to be hard mouthed, if he persists in gripping his dummies very tightly, or mouths or chews them on the way back to his handler. However, there is no real way of being sure until the dog is actually tried out on birds, and it is very sad when a dog has to be discarded for this fault at such a late stage of training.

12 The Great Day (University)

A puppy born in the spring should be ready to start his real job in life in the autumn of the following year, if no serious snags have occurred in training. Many owners, in fact, will be tempted to take their puppies out in January, when they may only be nine or ten months old. This temptation is best avoided, certainly by the shooting man, who will not be free to give the puppy the complete concentration needed. Mrs Purbrick does not think a gun should take his dog into the shooting field before he is three years old. Mr R. Baldwin says that two and a half is plenty young enough to start a dog on big shoots. However, most people, although agreeing that this is excellent advice, will have insufficient patience to carry it out.

A non-shooting gundog owner, who merely picks up and never shoots over his or her own dog, is in a slightly different category. If the pup's whistle control and steadiness are 100 per cent satisfactory, and his temperament is fairly phlegmatic, no harm is likely to be done by an early introduction to a day's shooting, provided it is a small day on which not enough will be shot to get the pup over-excited. Every care must be taken that he is not asked to retrieve anything which is not completely dead, as an immature dog might be tempted to nip a struggling bird, with disastrous consequences to the future quality of his mouth.

Puppies can also be taken out 'picking up cold' on the day following a shoot. The advantages are that there is no actual shooting to scare or excite the pup, and dead game will be thin on the ground and take a lot of finding. With a youngster which is easily bored or tired, of course, it would be a great mistake to try and make him hunt too long without a retrieve.

On some estates a great many unshot birds will have moved back into the coverts and, if game is too thick on the ground, the puppy is probably best left at home, as he will not always be in the handler's sight when he flushes something. It is always possible, too, that the pup may encounter a runner when he is too young and inexperienced to know what to do about it.

The shooting owner will probably wish to take his puppy out pigeon or rabbit shooting during the summer, when he will be twelve to eighteen months old. This will do no harm provided that he is ready—ie his training has progressed to the point reached in the last chapter—and that he is not asked to do too much. Rabbit shooting should be looked upon more as an exercise in steadiness than one in retrieving, as it is bad policy to send a young dog for a rabbit or hare he has seen running. If this is done it will suggest to the dog that fur is worth chasing. Even worse, of course, is to shoot at a rabbit or hare that a dog is already chasing. Not only is it dangerous, but if the quarry conveniently drops dead in front of the dog he will be likely to chase for evermore in the hope that the same thing will happen again. Naturally the trainer will not be in a position to punish the dog as he will return with a retrieve in his mouth. In a case like this it would make better sense psychologically to shoot the dog rather than the rabbit!

Pigeon shooting can be very good for young dogs, if they have shown that they will retrieve a cold pigeon without objecting too much to the loose feathers. If they are at all gun-nervous, they will dislike being in a hide with the gun, so this situation should be avoided. Otherwise, it is very good for the young dog to be made to wait a considerable time, while birds are dropped around him, before being allowed to retrieve. The handler should first clear the ground of any birds which are too close to make sensible retrieves. Two or three are ample for the dog on the first occasion.

Those lucky enough to have grouse shooting or picking up will find it an ideal opportunity to start their young dogs. The long waits will help teach the dog patience, and the fact that the birds take a lot of finding if they fall into deep heather will teach him to hunt persistently. On the other hand, it is not a good idea to keep a young dog hunting for a very long time for a bird unless one is absolutely certain that it is there, especially in hot weather. The last thing one wishes to do is to exhaust a youngster with unsuccessful hunts. Pickers-up on grouse moors can often get far enough behind the line to be able to practise their young entry on handling out for birds which drop out of the packs far behind the butts. These can be picked during the drive if one is out of sight and earshot.

A note of caution should be sounded on the subject of grouse shoots and young dogs. Everyone—guns, loaders, beaters, and pickers-up—is so keen after the long spring and summer break that there is a tendency for all to converge on any likely area as soon as each drive is over. This does not matter so much with old, experienced dogs which will carry on hunting despite all the distractions; but it is extremely bad for puppies, which are likely either to follow an older dog, thus preventing him from doing his job properly, or at least to become progressively more deaf to their owners' whistles. In theory a dog should be able to distinguish the sound of his own handler's whistle, because even if more than one of exactly the same make are being used, no two people blow them in exactly the same way. However, this is a distinction few excited youngsters will be capable of making, and one only has to stand still and listen between grouse drives to realise that the air is filled with whistling and shouting, all most confusing to the young dog. It will either cause him to refuse to hunt at all or teach him to ignore whistles and commands completely.

Mr Bob Baldwin is most emphatic that one should never let a young dog hunt where other people are hunting their dogs. If, when working two dogs oneself, the younger insists on following the older, one should make him sit and watch, keeping him for the easier retrieves where the precise location of the bird is known.

If circumstances make it more convenient to start the young dog off on a pheasant shoot, a day should be chosen when not much is likely to be shot and if the owner can persuade himself to leave his gun at home so much the better. Partridge shoots are even more suitable, but there are not many areas where they take place nowadays.

If the dog is not at all afraid of gunfire, the handler can station himself beside a gun and should then concentrate upon the dog and nothing else. He should not be on a lead. If it is necessary to have him tethered, he is not ready to be taken out shooting. There is no reason to suppose that he is any more likely to run in to the first bird he sees shot than to a dummy, as he will not know the difference. It is only later on, as the dog becomes more experienced, that he is liable to forget his steadiness.

It is far better for the handler to leave the youngster sitting and go and pick by hand any birds which fall in the open. The dog can be sent for one or two per drive at the most, but only those which fall in cover, or those he has not marked. The fewer marked birds he retrieves the better, as the fault of running in develops from anticipation of being sent for a bird he has seen fall.

Certainly the youngster should not be sent for any runners. Mr Male considers that many young dogs are made hard mouthed by being sent for live birds too soon. The handler is put into a difficult position if a gun shoots a bird which legs it into cover and the gun then asks him to send his dog. The handler should make a careful choice of neighbour, and explain that his dog is a youngster on its first outing and not capable yet of picking runners. Presumably mature dogs will be present to do the picking up, as the puppy handler should have made it plain to the owner of the shoot that his dog is merely coming out for experience and will not be of much practical value.

In this context, the trainer may wonder whether to bring out an older dog with his puppy or not. Provided that the older dog is reasonably well behaved (it need not be rock steady, as the handler can have it on a lead) and particularly that it does not whine, no harm will be done, and at least a dog will be available to send for runners. Whining is said to be very catching and therefore the last thing the handler of a young dog should do is to position himself anywhere near a dog which does it. Any tendency on the part of his own dog to whine must be sternly checked as soon as it starts. Some young dogs will whine the first time or two they are taken out, from cold, boredom or anxiety. This is completely different from the sort of whining done by a dog which has learnt what the game is all about and cannot control his excitement. Most trainers consider the latter sort of whining virtually incurable, but there is a variety of methods which can be tried before either discarding the dog or deciding to live with the fault and learn to endure it. Whining, like most faults, tends to worsen with age and the young dog which lets out the occasional squeak is likely to deteriorate into the ten-year-old that can be heard two fields away!

A real whiner is so excited that it probably does not know what it is doing, and punishment only tends to put it in a greater frenzy. However, before things get to this stage, it is worth trying a few of the dodges that have been known to work on some dogs. One is to remove one's hat with a swift movement unseen by the dog, and envelop his head with it in one hard, silent swipe. Some people advocate a squeezy bottle filled with water, to give the dog a squirt at every squeak. Others even recommend a soda syphon!

Dogs which start to whine at a heavy drive, when birds are falling all round them, may be helped by being taken to clay pigeon shoots, where they will encounter a constant barrage of gunfire and see 'birds' dropping all round them, but never get a retrieve. Eventually they may get bored with the performance and calm down.

130

It is possible that some dogs whine on such a high frequency that it cannot be heard by a human ear. If this is true it shows what a very complex subject it is and how difficult to cure, as obviously the dog will not know the difference between whining on a high or low frequency.

Mr Bob Baldwin recommends keeping the young dog really close to one from the outset, with a string or bootlace round his neck so that he can be grabbed and shaken if he starts. He recommends constant nagging, although some trainers disagree and advise dead silence.

Mr Eric Baldwin maintains that a whining dog should never be beaten, as that would only make matters worse. Eventually the dog becomes punch-drunk and impervious to punishment.

Mrs Jessel is of the opinion that whining can be prevented by never letting the young dog retrieve a marked bird. She believes in giving dogs very little to do in their first season.

An excitable dog should be given nothing to get excited about for as long as possible at the start of his career. That is to say, he should be made to sit and wait and be given the very minimum to do. If he calms down to the point of boredom, so much the better.

It is to be hoped that the youngster has already had the opportunity of retrieving various forms of cold game, but if not it is inadvisable to send him for a freshly shot bird in case he refuses to pick it up. It is far better to wait until a bird is available for the handler to throw for the dog at a suitable moment when nobody is looking, or drop it and send the dog back for it.

Use should be made in this way of anything which forms part of the bag and which one's puppy has never retrieved before. I always keep an eye on the game cart and give my young dogs a retrieve with every new species which appears. Then, the first time it is necessary to hunt—for instance, for a woodcock—one at least knows that the dog is prepared to pick it up if he comes across it.

Later on, difficulty may be experienced in getting the dog to

131

pick up live birds. The only thing to do in this case is to work up gradually from freshly shot, warm, dead birds to those which although dead still have a flutter left in them, and so on. Watching another dog retrieve runners will sometimes do the trick, especially if the handler takes the bird from the older dog's mouth, kills it, then immediately throws it for the younger dog to fetch. It is most unlikely that the youngster will continue long in his dislike of live birds. One young dog I had, by a famous Field Trial Champion, refused to pick up his first few live birds. In fact he caused me acute embarrassment on a grouse moor by finding a strong runner at some distance from me, in full view of the gun who had shot it, and refusing to pick it up. By the time I could get there with the other dogs, the bird had disappeared, never to be seen again. However, before the end of his first season he was a different dog and continually turning up with runners which other dogs had failed to find.

It should be realised that it is quite a problem for the youngster to distinguish between an unshot bird which he must not chase and a strong runner which he may. The key, of course, is the blood scent which a wounded bird will emit and an unshot one will not. It naturally takes time for a gundog to learn the distinction.

Although it is always galling to lose birds, it is better for a young dog to be diffident about chasing runners than to be too keen. He has plenty of time to learn. I once entered a young dog in a trial, assuming that he retrieved runners all right as he had brought me back several live birds from cover. For his first retrieve he was sent across a river to find a bird which had been seen to run into a thick bramble patch. He crossed the river and entered the cover, whereupon the bird emerged and legged it along the river bank. The dog stood and watched it, with an expression on his face which clearly said, 'What a good boy am I!' Unfortunately, the bird had too good a start and was never found. It certainly taught me not to assume a dog is capable of taking a line and catching a lively runner unless I have actually seen him do it. Picking up live birds which have tucked in is not the same thing at all.

In another trial, a puppy was easily eyewiped by an experienced dog when she had taken the line of a runner a considerable distance into tall bracken, after which the bird was seen to fly above the bracken for a few yards. In spite of vocal encouragement, the puppy returned without the bird, obviously having thought that as it could fly it was not the one she was looking for. The experienced dog had watched this performance and thus knew exactly where to find the bird, which did not fly again and remained in the same patch of bracken.

The more experienced a dog becomes, the more likely it is to run in, having learnt what fun retrieving the real thing is. The handler must be on constant guard against this and not send his young dog to retrieve too quickly, and not for too many birds. He should still try to pick more himself than the number for which he sends his dog. There is a danger too in establishing in one's mind a minimum distance at which it is worth sending the dog for a retrieve. The dog will quickly learn this critical distance and, although he may be rock steady on birds dropping really close, he may tend to run in on birds beyond what he has come to regard as likely retrieving distance. If one's dog has marked a bird a long way down the line, it is tempting to send him for it (provided the gun concerned has no dog), but it is far better to let someone else have the retrieve and stick as far as possible to the rule of 'no marked birds in the open'. Of course, there comes a time when one has to send a dog after a runner very quickly rather than risk losing the bird. However, it must be remembered that such an action is always detrimental to a dog's training. The reason why some older dogs, whose discipline otherwise is fairly intact, will run in on runners only is not that they have worked out that runners are likely to escape, but that they have learnt to expect to be sent for them without delay.

Mr Male's opinion is that shooting is what ruins a well-trained dog! The worst bird to send a young dog for is the one thought to be dead but which flies when the dog gets to it.

If, after all this careful training and gentle introduction to game, one's young hopeful turns out to be hard mouthed, little can be done. A hard-mouthed dog is not one which tears the occasional bird. This damage may be done in the act of catching a lively runner, or dragging it out of brambles. The running cock which comes to hand tailless, or with a patch of feathers missing from its back, is evidence of care on the part of the dog rather than the reverse. A hard-mouthed dog crushes the ribs of a bird, without necessarily doing any visible damage at all. Birds must be felt to discover whether they are damaged and, if the dog persistently brings in birds whose ribs are crushed on one or both sides, he is almost certainly hard mouthed. Some birds are damaged by the shot, or by hitting trees or hard ground in their descent, so the odd bird with its ribs in should not necessarily be blamed on the dog.

On an outside or cock shooting day at the beginning or end of the season it is quite possible that nothing suitable for the puppy's first retrieve will be shot all day. This does not matter. A bird can be borrowed and planted for the dog to retrieve, but this is not really necessary. His early days out shooting can be utilised to teach many lessons that have no connection with retrieving. The foundation for good manners both during and between drives will have been laid in dummy work, but the finishing touches have still to be made. The trainer must make sure that his charge sits quietly and patiently during drives and walks to heel between them, instead of running off to play with other dogs or diving into any available cover. It is too much to expect a young dog to behave all day like an old stager without once letting off steam, so the opportunity should be taken once or twice, where and when he can do no damage, to let him run about briefly. During long drives, too, the handler can and should unbend to the extent of giving the youngster some petting and kind words at times when there is nothing much happening.

The finished gundog must learn to get in and out of a variety of strange vehicles, and to sit and wait while his master and others negotiate fences.

It is essential that the trainer should pick very carefully the sort of shoot to which he first takes his young dog, and avoid anywhere where the other dogs are likely to be totally uncontrolled and rush about picking up every bird that falls. Having gone to the trouble of training his first youngster, the gun may well feel that he no longer wishes to take part in such shoots, if by so doing he has either to leave his dog at home or risk wasting all his hard work. Alternatively, he may find that he can make converts by demonstrating the joy and practicality of owning a well-trained dog. It would be a really worth-while achievement to raise the general standard of gundog training in one's area by showing that it is not difficult to produce a well-behaved and thoroughly useful dog, even without previous experience.

13 Living Happily Ever After

Gradually the young dog will become of more use to his owner as he gains in experience, but too much must not be expected too soon. Many owners tend to compare their youngsters unfavourably with their old stagers, forgetting that it took several years for the old dog to learn all that makes him so useful today. Most retrievers are of limited value until their second season, depending upon the talents of the individual dog and possibly even more upon the amount of experience they receive. Naturally a dog which goes out once a week on the type of shoot where pickers-up do most of the work will end the season having learnt far less than if he belonged to a man who shot three or four days every week or to a picker-up who worked his dogs an equal amount.

A dog should never stop being trained for the whole of his life. He is not a machine which, once set, will work without further adjustment. There is always a delicate balance to be kept between the desire not to lose a single bird that is shot and the wish not to ruin the dog. It is always a mistake, from the point of view of the dog's training, to send him for a runner too quickly, but on the other hand many runners can be lost by delay. The gun on a formal shoot with an inexperienced dog should arrange for a picker-up to be handy to deal with the birds for which he does not wish to send his dog, and on a rough shoot should try to ensure that at least some of his companions have competent dogs.

To make sure that one's trained dog remains trained, it is necessary to be a dog man first and a shooting man second. Because so few shooting people put their priorities in this order, the standard of dog work on most shoots is appallingly, and unnecessarily, low. One learns to take it for granted that at least three-quarters of the guns' dogs will have to be pegged during drives and, if they are released and set off after the wrong bird, no power on earth will stop them. Worse still is the dog which is sent for one bird, picks it, then sees another shot and rushes off after it, dropping the bird he has in his mouth. When one of these menaces has been loose during a drive it is impossible to know what has been picked and what has not and birds are liable to be left behind.

The man who has taken trouble to train his dog carefully and thoroughly, therefore, can gain a great deal of pleasure not only from the performance of his dog, but from the respect and admiration he will receive from his friends. To take an extreme case, I once sold a young bitch with field trial awards to a man whose shooting companions had never seen a steady dog before and could not get over it. The result was not that they all went home and trained their own dogs, but that they formed a queue for the bitch's puppies, as if they expected them to be born trained!

In many ways the non-shooting gundog owner is in a better position to keep his dog on the straight and narrow, if only for the reason that he has nothing else but his dog to think about. So often one sees someone shoot a bird and only notice that his dog has taken off after it when it is too late to stop him. I once sold a young dog which was dummy trained but not experienced. He was quiet and biddable, and the easiest possible type to keep steady. However, when his owner was shooting over him all his concentration was on the birds and none on his dog. The latter started to rise to his feet when a bird was shot, from which it was a very short step to running in. During the summer following his first season, the dog was sent for a refresher course to another trainer, who could achieve nothing because the dog behaved perfectly for him, as he would have done for anybody willing to keep one eye on him and check instantly any movement from the sitting position.

A dog very quickly learns when his master is concentrating upon him and when he is not. The minute the handler's concentration wanders, the dog will take advantage of it. A dog-minded shooter will master the art of checking on his dog at all times, without necessarily missing the chance of shooting at birds that come over him, although he will recognise that it is better to miss one or two opportunities than to spoil a good dog.

On the other hand, the first time the trainer actually shoots over his own dog, the latter's respect for him will grow enormously, and a new dimension will be added to their partnership. Previously the dog will not have realised his master to be capable of shooting birds for him.

If the amateur trainer reaches the end of his dog's first season without him having committed any major crimes, still steady, and having at least made a start at being really useful in the matter of finding runners and other difficult birds, he may congratulate himself. The battle is far from over, however. The dog will *always* be inclined to run in and chase, for that is the nature of a dog. Once the season is over, he should not metaphorically be put away in a cupboard in the same way as the owner's shotgun. Mr Clitheroe remarks that far too many people turn their gundogs over to the household for the summer and expect them to function properly when the season comes round. He likes the owner to have his dog with him as much as possible and to take every opportunity of keeping him obedient. For instance, if the dog is told to sit, it is essential to make sure that he stays.

Mrs Purbrick is of the opinion that a gundog should not be allowed complete freedom to wander about the house until he is five. She recommends leaving him in the kennel when the owner is not free actively to concentrate upon him. In her opinion the two essential virtues for a shooting man's dog are steadiness and willingness to return instantly when called. It is highly embarrassing on a formal shoot for a gun to be unable to move on to the next drive, which may be such a long way away it is necessary for the party to travel in Land-rovers, because his dog is missing and will not return. Mr Clitheroe prizes as one of the greatest virtues of F.T.Ch. Hedenhampark Holcot Fay, whose outstanding record includes winning the Retriever Championship twice, the fact that she will always reappear from a wood the first time she is whistled.

After one or two seasons of being used purely as a retriever, some guns may wish to use the same dog for hunting up hedgerows etc. Provided that discipline has been fully maintained, so that the dog will still stop instantly on the whistle and take directions, no harm should be done. Many experienced trainers use their older dogs for beating or hunting up. Mrs Radclyffe has one which will work a grouse moor, and point and back like a pointer. However, she would not try it with a youngster.

Many shooters with a well-trained dog eventually come to enjoy working their dogs as much as, or more than, their shooting. They may then wish to go out picking up on their non-shooting days. Alternatively, there are plenty of people, especially women, who have no interest in shooting as such but who thoroughly enjoy training and working gundogs. They will soon find that it is almost impossible to do a really efficient job with only one dog, particularly if it is an inexperienced youngster. Once they are in the position of having several dogs with them it is a lot easier not to spoil the current young hopeful. A team might comprise the youngster which must not be spoilt on any account, and which would be unlikely to find a strong runner anyway; the current trial dog (if the owner is trial minded) which can be sent for some runners, as he will be in trials; and the old stager, retired from competition, who gets all the dirty work. The single-dog owner is in a very difficult situation if he is picking up and thus occupying a position which could be taken by somebody out to fill his host's bag, rather than train his dog!

Picking up is like so many things in that it is extremely hard to break into the charmed circle, but, once one has built up a reputation for having efficient and well-disciplined dogs, more invitations are likely to follow. It is hardly surprising that no one wishes to take on an unknown quantity in the form of an inexperienced dog and handler, but everyone was a beginner once and the really keen amateur will sooner or later find a friendly keeper or shoot owner prepared to give him a trial.

Shoots vary enormously in the way their picking up is organised, between those which do not seem to care if their birds are recovered or not and those which make certain before each shooting day that they have an experienced team who are used to working together and each of whom probably has his favourite position for every drive. Most pickers-up prefer the sort of shoot where it is possible to mark and account for every bird, rather than the kind where the amount of game shot necessitates a 'carpet-sweeping' operation which one can never be certain of having finished.

Very heavily wooded shoots present problems, in that it is not possible to stand well back or one would see nothing. When standing with the guns it is only possible to estimate the general line of flight of a pricked bird which carries on over the treetops, and some are inevitably lost.

In more open country the ideal position for the picker-up is well back, out of shot or behind a thick tree or building. Many birds will thus be picked which the guns may not realise were hit, and after the drive the pickers-up can walk forward and help the guns look for any remaining birds which fell near them.

In order to be asked again, pickers-up should remember not to collect any birds shot by guns who have their own dogs, unless they are asked to do so, except in the case of pricked birds falling well back when it is probably not possible to know which gun was responsible. On the other hand, nothing is more trying to the picker-up, or more of a strain on his or her good manners, than to asked to look for a long-departed runner on ground foiled by guns and inefficient dogs, when he knows that his dog could have retrieved it quite easily had he been asked to do so in time.

140

The picker-up should also remember to ask which woods are being driven during the day, so that he does not commit the faux pas of pursuing a strong runner right through the next drive, scattering birds in all directions. Actually, I have a suspicion that an *experienced* dog well and truly on the line of a runner on a good scenting day does very little damage, but few keepers and shoot owners are of the same opinion, so their wishes must be respected. Of course, after the next drive has taken place, not only will the line of the runner be cold but will have been obliterated by the beaters, so it is only possible to find the bird later by doing a carpet-sweep and hoping to come across it. This will usually entail missing most, if not all, of the next drive.

One bird of this sort found and added to the bag is worth a dozen of the easy ones which should have been left for the guns to pick either with their own dogs or by hand. Few people are more unpopular than the sort of picker-up who rushes about in full view collecting the maximum number of birds in the minimum time, leaving the others to trek after the one which was seen to collapse a couple of fields away, or the one which no one else noticed at all. Good pickers-up at work should be unobtrusive, but they should let the guns know what they have picked, and the keeper or host, or both, what they have failed to find.

The gundog which gives his owner so much pleasure and satisfaction deserves every care and consideration. Therefore the owner's first task on returning home after a day's shooting is to ensure that his dog is warm, dry, fed and watered, before attending to his own comfort or even to the cleaning of his gun. If the dog is very muddy, it is a good idea to try and get the worst off by letting him have a swim in any available water before putting him into the car. Some owners make a point of drying their dogs before setting off for home, but this is not really necessary in the case of an estate car where the dog can be put in the back with plenty of newspaper to roll about in. On a journey of half an hour or so it will be found that he will have more or less dried himself.

Attention to such points as these will help to ensure that the dog does not become prematurely affected with rheumatics, but old dogs which are a bit stiff and uncomfortable the following day can be helped by the administration of one or two Disprin at bedtime on the day of a shoot.

Mr Eric Baldwin expresses himself very forthrightly on the subject of owners who do not treat their dogs with sufficient thought and consideration, and I am in total agreement with him. He lets his kennel dogs out five times a day and strongly disapproves of people who leave theirs shut up from 6pm until the following morning. It is to be hoped that, in the process of training, the owner has come to enjoy the company of his dog for its own sake, and thus will not wish to neglect him either during or between seasons. The companionship of a responsive trained dog is a very wonderful thing, impossible to explain to someone who has never experienced it.

The dog should be kept fit, hard and well disciplined between seasons. It is no use training a dog and working him carefully through one season, only to let him run wild and go off and chase rabbits all the summer. Equally it is foolish to let him get fat and lazy, if only because the lives of fat dogs are inevitably shortened and made less healthy and happy. Retrievers nearly always want to eat far more than is good for them and, if the dog is fat on what may seem to be a spartan ration, the simple answer is that he is still getting too much. More exercise will help, up to a point, but with fat dogs as with fat people there is only one real answer: less food! To quote Mrs Purbrick, 'If only people would realise that to have a happy dog is to have a thin dog, to have a disciplined dog and a dog which knows its job.'

It is a good idea to have a few sessions with the dummy during the summer, unless one is unlucky enough to have the sort of dog which refuses to have anything to do with dummies the minute he has experienced the real thing. In these cases the only answer is to keep the dog fit, well exercised and well disciplined, to try to take him pigeon shooting once or twice, and to watch him extra carefully at the start of the next season. All dogs, in fact, are likely to think they know it all at the start of their second season, and be inclined to 'try it on'. The handler should be ready for this and act accordingly.

Dogs vary not only in how long they are likely to live, but in how active they remain into old age. This is a point well worth considering in the original purchase of a dog. If several of his ancestors are still fit and working at an advanced age, there is a good chance that he, given equal care, may do the same. Many inexperienced owners are puzzled as to how old is 'old' and the ancient tradition equating every year of a dog's life to seven years of a man's is not much help. Obviously a yearling dog, being fully grown and able to reproduce, can in no way be compared with a seven-year-old child, and equally obviously more dogs reach the age of sixteen than people the age of 112. The following table makes due allowance for the comparatively short 'childhood' of a dog, and may prove a useful rule-of-thumb guide:

A dog of 3 months	equals a human of	5	years
,, ,, 6 months	,, ,, ,,	10	,,
,, ,, 9 months	,, ,, ,,	12½	,,
,, ,, 1 year	,, ,, ,,	15	,,
,, ,, 18 months	,, ,, ,,	20	,,
,, ,, 2 years	,, ,, ,,	25	,,
,, ,, 3 years	,, ,, ,,	30	,,
,, ,, 4 years	,, ,, ,,	35	,,

and so on, adding five years for every year of the dog's life, ending with a human centenarian equalling a seventeen-year-old dog.

However fit an old dog is, if a particular owner's shooting is very strenuous, he cannot be expected to work hard all day towards the end of his life. However, a member of a formal shoot where most of the work is done by pickers-up is likely to be able to bring his dog out into extreme old age. A dog can often manage a half-day whereas he could not cope with a long one, and as gundogs enjoy their work so much it seems a pity to leave them at home the whole time until it becomes absolutely necessary.

It is advisable for the owner to start thinking about a replacement in plenty of time, remembering that, if he wishes to buy a young puppy and train it himself, at least two years will elapse before the youngster will be of much use. Therefore, if the present dog is beginning to show signs of slowing down at the age of eight or nine, the time has probably come to invest in a new puppy. Few adult dogs resent the advent of another dog into the household, although many owners expect them to. On the contrary, the arrival of a puppy often knocks years off the old one, who really welcomes the companionship.

Plate 27   Most older retrievers are tolerant with young puppies

Although most retrievers are benevolent and long-suffering with young puppies, some tact must be exercised at first, and certainly the puppy should not be left alone with the old dog until it is certain that the latter is to be trusted with him. Many dogs (and some bitches) hate the way a young puppy will rush up to them and investigate their underparts looking for a milk supply, and until the pup has got over this phase it is as well to keep them apart. It is an interesting fact that the majority of blind owners of guide dogs (which are mainly retrievers, chosen among other things for their kindly temperaments), keep their old dog as a pet after it has become necessary for a younger one to take its place, and resentment is hardly ever shown, although naturally the young dog is the one to accompany the owner everywhere, while the pensioner has to stay at home.

It is, admittedly, distressing for both owner and dog the first time it has to be decided that the old stager is no longer fit to go out shooting, even for half a day; but, once master has left, the pensioner is likely to settle contentedly in front of the fire. This must be kinder than subjecting him to wet, cold, stress and exhaustion that he is no longer able to stand.

It should not be assumed that the training of the second dog will proceed without problems, any more than that of the first is likely to have done. Certainly the trainer should have profited by his mistakes and be determined not to repeat them, but it is all too easy to make a completely different set of mistakes with the second dog. It can be a case of a little learning being a dangerous thing. Training a dog can be likened to the making of a soufflé. The first attempt is likely to be successful, as the beginner will adhere strictly to the recipe and do exactly what the book says. However, the next time over-confidence may cause the result to be a flop.

Even the most experienced trainers state unanimously that they are still learning.

145

14 Field Trials and Working Tests

Selfishly, one is tempted not to enlarge upon the pleasures of taking part in competitions with a home-trained dog. Field trials are already grossly over-subscribed to the extent that many stakes have at least three times more applicants than can be admitted. Working tests have not yet arrived at the same stage, but as trial grounds become harder and harder to come by and the expenses of trialling continue to rise, tests may eventually receive similar pressure.

These days, most people enter the sport of field trialling via working tests, and opinions are divided as to whether or not this is a good thing. There is a violent anti-working-test lobby, which is of the opinion that artificial tests on dummies or cold game do nothing but harm to the genuine working gundog movement. However, nearly all the trainers interviewed for this book hold the opposite view: that so long as working tests are not given undue importance, and so long as the general puppy-buying and stud dog-using public is not deceived about the difference between tests and trials, they do no harm. In fact, they do positive good. The would-be field trialler may have reached the stage where his dog is far above the standard reached by any other on the shoots to which he has access, but working tests can still perform a valuable service by showing him how he is likely to get on under competition conditions, on strange ground, and with a variety of more complicated retrieves than one would get on a shooting day. If, out shooting, a bird falls on the far side of an almost impenetrable hedge, the average handler would either go right up to the hedge to urge the dog through it, or would find a gap. At a

Plate 28 Mrs Radclyffe encouraging a young Labrador to negotiate a
thick hedge

trial the dog would be expected to tackle the obstacle with the
handler standing well back. Very little time can be wasted on a
shooting day in practising one's dog for such eventualities—
that is where training classes and tests can be so valuable.

Most ardent triallists, when asked their opinion of working
tests, reply that they see no harm in them provided they are
regarded as a means to an end and not an end in themselves,
and also provided that handlers do not keep special dogs for
tests. The latter description includes the spectacular performer
that is uncontrollable on game, the whiner and the hard
mouthed. In practice, however, very few of the most successful
working-test dogs are not also successful field triallers.

Such is the pressure on the countryside today that few
buyers of retriever puppies can ever hope to give them their

proper job to do. This is a pity, and some would use stronger words. However, the fact remains that the vast majority of retrievers born today have no chance of doing the work for which they were bred. It seems preferable that their and their owners' lives should be enhanced by doing some sort of training together, and working tests provide a valuable outlet for the pet owner who wishes to utilise the inborn working instincts of his or her dog in some way, and at the same time to give himself a rewarding pastime which will take him into the countryside at weekends and make him a host of new friends with similar interests. Most of those who condemn tests so roundly are people with unlimited access to the countryside and to shooting, so their attitude could be thought to be a little selfish.

The novice wishing to enter his first working test should join one or two of his local gundog clubs, and preferably attend training classes first. Most clubs run either a puppy/novice working test, or separate tests for puppies and novices. The definition of a puppy is usually a youngster of less than two years, and a novice a dog which has not won any award in a field trial or open working test or a first prize in any other test. A few clubs run novice dog and handler tests, in which the handler, too, must not previously have won.

Such tests normally comprise four or five exercises, nearly always commencing with a walk-up of several dogs in line together off the lead, each to retrieve a marked dummy in turn. Points are given for accurate marking, speed, delivery and good heel-keeping. No bonus points are awarded for steadiness, which is considered essential, and all marks are likely to be lost if the dog runs in.

The other tests will usually include a retrieve of an unseen dummy, in which the handler is given a description of the dummy's position and the dog is tested on his ability to stop on the whistle and take directions. Marked retrieves from cover, over a jump, and across or from water are the most common additions.

148

Any young dog which is intended to be taken out shooting in the season following should be able to take part in one of these summer tests without disgracing himself or his handler.

Open working tests are of slightly more dubious value, as few competitors can pretend that they are taking part in them for the benefit of the dog's education. Most canine competitors in open tests have at least one season's experience, and many of them continue taking part in them for years, especially if they are the type of dogs which retain a life-long enthusiasm for dummies. However, there can be little objection to gundog owners having an enjoyable get-together out of season and some practice for their dogs; the fact that this takes the form of a competition adds extra interest.

Organisers and judges of working tests should resist the temptation to resort to gimmicks and tricks to sort out the dogs. It should be perfectly possible to judge them on a set of straightforward, practical exercises by taking account of style, handleability and other positive virtues. It is so much pleasanter for all concerned to judge dogs upon what they can do rather than upon what they cannot do.

Open working-test exercises generally feature a high proportion of unseen to marked dummies. Double or treble retrieves, mock drives, thick cover, and long swims are frequently encountered. A typical test might include a walk-up with either a marked double dummy, the dog to retrieve both in the order chosen by the judge, or a marked dummy in front and an unseen behind the line, the latter to be collected first. The next exercise might be an unseen retrieve over a jump, with a mock 'running rabbit' (a fur dummy on a pulley) crossing the dog's path at some stage. Other likely exercises are unseen retrieves from cover, beyond hedges, or on water.

Working tests such as these are arranged to entertain and instruct the public at game fairs and similar events. This means that compromise has to be struck between a fair competition for the dogs and a readily understood spectacle for the public, not always an easy task.

A dog which can acquit himself creditably at a working test of good standard, is a thoroughly useful dog out shooting, and has no major faults, may be a likely field trial prospect.

Field trials are run as nearly as possible on the lines of a day's shooting, except that the emphasis is on the dog work and not on the size of the bag, which is inevitably smaller than would normally be the case on the same ground. This is partly because less time can be spent actually shooting, owing to the fact that each bird must be picked individually and the dog concerned given a fair chance.

One-day stakes normally cater for twelve to fifteen runners, and can be for novice dogs and/or handlers, or puppies and non-winners. One-day open stakes are restricted to twelve dogs, whereas two-day open stakes cater for twenty-four. Nominations are decided by ballot, club members always receiving preference. In practice this means that, in order to get into about six trials per year of any category, it is probably necessary to belong to twelve or eighteen societies, depending upon the part of the country in which one lives.

There are basically two ways of conducting a retriever trial, either by walking up or by having drives, or the two can be combined on some estates. Certainly walked-up trials are easier and more satisfactory to judge, in that everyone has a chance of seeing each bird down, and a dog is usually sent immediately a bird is shot. When the trial is being run on drives there is always the danger of eliminating a dog for failing on a bird which may have been picked by another dog, or have got up and run twenty minutes before the dog was put on to it. If there is enough game, most judges will take this sort of thing into consideration and only penalise a dog for failing on a bird subsequently picked from the area in which the handler was told to try his dog. Sometimes, for various reasons, game is in very short supply, and judges are forced to use any excuse to eliminate a dog in order to bring the trial to a conclusion.

It is highly desirable to test dogs for steadiness and silence at drives, but most triallists prefer a preponderance of walking up. In order to qualify for the title of Field Trial Champion, dogs now have not only to win two open stakes, but to have passed a water test and sat quietly at a drive, so estates with facilities for both these tests are now in greater demand than ever.

There are normally either three or four judges at Retriever Field Trials. When there are three, each officiates individually with two dogs and handlers under his eye at any one time, until the final stages of the trial when the judges make their decisions together. When there are four judges they work in pairs, still with two dogs and handlers to each pair. There are usually six guns, two to each judge, or three to each pair under the four-judge system.

Dogs are called into line in numerical order and normally given two retrieves per round, perhaps only one if game is scarce or the dog has been particularly unimpressive. After each dog that has not disgraced itself has been through two or three rounds, depending upon conditions, some of them are chosen to take part in further rounds until a decision can be reached.

Naturally, in a trial being run realistically on game, it is impossible to give the dogs equal opportunities. Judges take account of this, but it is true that to win trials one requires luck as well as a good dog. It is almost as frustrating to go through a trial with nothing but easy birds, so that one's dog has no opportunity to shine, as it is to be asked, first dog down, to retrieve an almost impossible runner and to be eliminated for failing to do so.

Part of the fascination of field trials lies in their uncertainty. Probably everyone being called into line, particularly for the first time in any trial, will feel extremely nervous, but the satisfaction to be obtained from a good performance by one's dog, and the unstinted congratulations invariably given by one's fellow competitors, make all the anguish worth while.

Equally, other handlers are always ready with sincere sympathy when things go wrong. The occasional thrilling win keeps one going in the hope of another, and helps one to forget the occasions when the judges were felt to be unfair or the dog let one down in some spectacular way. I can honestly say that out of well over a hundred trials, there was only one in which I still think the judges were blatantly unfair to my dog, and that was an occasion where game was extremely scarce on the first day, creating great judging difficulties. However, plenty of dramatic exits from trials remain in my memory to be laughed at now, although they may not have seemed so amusing at the time. On one particular occasion I was afflicted by a sudden nosebleed when in line during the run-off of an important two-day open stake. My whistle silted up and the bitch was eliminated for being out of control, when she persisted in hunting for a partridge in completely the wrong place. Unfortunately, not only was my whistle useless, but my shouts went unheard owing to a noisy tractor in the next field.

There is nothing like field trialling for keeping one humble. I still cherish the memory of the handler who, after an exceptional run of successes in open stakes, was holding forth about what a comedown it was to be running in a non-winner stake again with a new dog. She was put firmly in her place, not by the other handlers, but by her dog taking off into the distance in a vast field of sugar beet, putting up birds in all directions. Fortunately the dog was recaptured before entirely clearing the trial ground of game, but the handler was no doubt taught a sharp lesson! Conversely, it is often the case that the handler lets the dog down rather than the other way about.

Anyone wishing to make a start in field trials would be well advised to visit one or two as a spectator before deciding whether or not his dog is up to the required standard. Kennel Club rules and their guide to field trial judges state clearly what is required of a field trial dog, and owners of prospective entrants should make a point of reading them. Briefly, the chief virtue for which the judges are looking is game-finding ability, followed by nose, marking ability, drive, style, speed, control and a good delivery. Eliminating faults are hardness of mouth, whining or barking, running in or chasing, being out of control or failing to enter water. Some other major faults are failure to find game, poor heelkeeping, disturbing unshot ground, noisy handling and changing birds.

Mrs Purbrick, who for many years was a field trial secretary as well as a competitor and judge, sounds a warning about the increasing difficulty of obtaining ground for field trials. The cost of a day's shooting is now so high that it is difficult to understand why any host should give it away. The only ones who do so are those inspired by an unselfish love of dogs and dog work, and a desire to make a contribution to the improvement of gundogs in general, or by loyalty to a particular breed or club. Competitors should always remember this and behave as guests, and under no circumstances audibly criticise the ground, the supply of game or the ability of the guns.

Mr Male remarks that it is easy to criticise trials and the way they are run, but it is indisputable that they have resulted in a great improvement in the general standard of dog work over the years.

Similar views are expressed by Mr Clitheroe, who thinks that the standard of dog work among keepers in his area has improved enormously, purely through an interest in field trials.

Mr R. Baldwin looks back to the days when a dog might have had up to sixteen retrieves in a one-day stake. Today it is occasionally possible for two two-day stakes to be won on a total of no more than ten retrieves. Neither does he think that some of today's Field Trial Champions could sit through a really hot drive.

Mrs Atkinson and Mrs Radclyffe both consider that too much attention is paid to faults at field trials, rather than judging in a more positive way by looking for virtues. They would not eliminate a dog for one small squeak or for hard mouth unless the evidence was overwhelming—a view shared by Mr E. Baldwin, who states that a dog should never be put out of a trial for hard mouth unless the judges have seen where the bird fell.

Mr Wylie feels that over the years the standard of both dogs and judging has improved. In particular, the dogs are handled a great deal better than they used to be. He has made a host of good friends through dogs and trials, finding that dog people on the whole are very sporting and do not bear grudges for long. The few who take the game too seriously do not normally last long in it.

It is to be hoped that new people coming into field trials will uphold the wonderfully sporting and friendly spirit which still prevails, and will never cease to show their gratitude and appreciation to the generous landowners without whom trials would cease to exist. All breeds of working gundog would be immeasurably the poorer if that sad day ever came.

Index